The Rise and Fall of H&H Bagels

By Marc Zirogiannis

Published by Revival Waves of Glory Books & Publishing
PO Box 596| Litchfield, Illinois 62056 USA
www.revivalwavesofgloryministries.com

Revival Waves of Glory Books & Publishing is committed to excellence in the publishing industry.

EBook: 978-1-62676-994-6

Paperback: 978-0692542835

Inquiries or additional information contact:

Marc A. Zirogiannis
338 Jericho Turnpike-ste 114
Syosset, NY 11791
Email: redflagadvisors@gmail.com

Or visit
www.marczirogiannis.com

PUBLISHED IN THE UNITED STATES OF AMERICA

FOR SORAYA

About the Author

Marc Zirogiannis holds a B.A. from Long Island University, and a *Juris Doctor* from Hofstra University's School of Law. Mr. Zirogiannis is a world renowned Business Development Consultant and Author. In 2014, he was nominated as "The Best Author on Long Island" by BOLI.

Mr. Zirogiannis has practiced the martial arts for over 25 years under the supervision of Grandmaster Yeon Hwan Park. He has been active in practicing and teaching meditation for 10 years. He has published numerous books, eBooks, and Audio Books on a variety of subjects, and, is currently the lead correspondent for ***Tae Kwon Do Times***, an international print publication. He lectures on a variety of topics, including business development, personal development, and matters of the martial arts.

His first major novel, **The Suffering of Innocents,** has been a major critical success, being lauded as "stunning, magnificent, and heart-wrenching" by Reader Views.

Table of Contents

Acknowledgements

Endless thanks for the love and support of my beloved Soraya, and my boys, DJ, Deme, Joseph and Sebastian. Without them, it all means nothing.

This book is dedicated to Norman Levy, the beloved icon of the frozen bagel business.

Thanks to Mallory Greene for her invaluable assistance in editing this work.

This book is a work of non-fiction that may evoke certain negative images of the characters featured. It is not an attempt to discredit any real individuals or institutions. It is an attempt to tell a story from my own unique and first person account of what occurred between 2009-2015 in the world of H&H Bagels. Others may, and probably do, have other versions of the stories presented in this work.

-Marc Zirogiannis

Introduction

In the summer of 2012, I had the opportunity to enjoy a lunch meeting with the owners of the Davidovich Bagel brand. They were in the process of becoming recognized as the heir-apparent to the bagel legacy left behind by the, then defunct, H&H Bagels.

Their product was still being made the traditional way, even for the wholesale market. These two entrepreneurs had captured much of the local and international business, as well as the name recognition, that had once belonged to Helmer Toro, the now dethroned bagel king of New York.

Most significantly, these individuals were a sharp contrast to the man I once worked for in the most notorious bagel company that ever existed. They were straight talking, square dealing, businessmen that were building their own brand and reputation the old fashioned way: through hard work.

Like everyone associated with the bagel business, they were intrigued by the downfall of H&H. After all, H&H was the standard bearer that most bagel companies compared themselves to as they were developing their business model and brand identity.

"So what really happened with H&H?" Gene, the more serious of the two men, inquired.

"I don't think we have enough time over one lunch to tell that story," I conjectured.

"Go ahead. We are in no rush. How does a business like that fail?" asked Michael, his partner and fellow Davidovich, in his distinct, Ukrainian accent.

I ordered myself a glass of wine, despite it being only lunchtime, and took a deep breath. I was about to retell a colorful and complex story that was, perhaps, unique in the history of modern business. It was the true story of a meteoric rise and tragic fall of a business that had to be experienced to be fully understood.

"Okay," I said. "I will tell you the story but you are never going to believe it."

Chapter 1

"We're the Google of Bagels." (**Helmer Toro**)

August, 2014- The day was as hot and uncomfortable as any August day to ride the New York City subway. Marcus stood, holding the rail, on the crowded #1 local, as the train raced downtown. He was struck by the fact that it had been quite a while since he had ridden this line. In fact, he couldn't remember exactly when he had ridden it last, but it must have been, at least, five years prior to this day.

As the train approached the stop, the announcer's voice rang out throughout the belly of the slowing car, "72nd Street, next stop. Watch the gap."

The train came to a screeching halt and, after a moment of hesitation, the doors slid open. A mass of New Yorkers pushed in and out of the car in the minimal time allotted for this exercise. For New Yorkers, this was nothing unusual. Navigation of the massive public transportation system in New York was sink or swim. Either you figured out the flow and protocol quickly, or you found yourself missing a lot of trains.

"Stand clear of the closing doors."

Just as Marcus heard the announcement he looked up towards the closing doors that were in his sight line, and he couldn't believe his eyes. Making his way through the crowd was an all too familiar face. How was it possible, with the millions of people being shepherded around the city every day that he would come face to face with the one man he hoped never to see again? That man was Helmer Toro.

Helmer was not only the most notorious bagel manufacturer in the world, he was also Marcus' former employer.

Now, after three years of having no communication, whatsoever, here they were, face to face. It was obvious that Helmer was as shocked as Marcus at the encounter. This, clearly, was a chance meeting. Neither man was prepared for it, but here they were.

Helmer stood before Marcus, looking virtually the same as when he last saw him.

His black, Bernie Madoff cap was pulled tightly onto his head. His glasses were thick and round. His pants were always khaki. His shirts, always flannel to keep his pigment-deprived skin from getting burnt. Most distinctly, he wore his nervous, little smile. Not a smile of joy. Not even a sinister smile. It was just a slightly perched, little smile. Both of his lips were pressed firmly together, with the ends turned slightly upwards, somewhat like a wooden marionette.

"Hey, Marcus. Good to see ya," Helmer said congenially as he extended his right hand. The "ya" in his sentenced lingered slightly as if it were stuck on his tongue.

Marcus looked down at Helmer's extended hand and did nothing. He had no intention of going through a charade of cordiality with this sociopath.

"Hey, kid. No hard feelings. That stuff was all business. We can still be friends."

At this point, Marcus realized he couldn't remain silent any longer.

"Helmer, let's be clear. We are not now, nor have we ever been friends. All I care about is getting my money. As for you, you are a cancer and if I never saw you again, it would be too soon."

Helmer immediately turned red. He was so used to being able to charm people, even his enemies; in fact, especially his enemies. He was so used to engendering a positive response that he didn't know what to do when he didn't receive one. He just stood there, beat red, with his hand out and said nothing as Marcus pushed past him.

As Marcus forged on and departed the train, he had no inkling that he would never see Helmer Toro again. At least, not in person. He turned back slightly to watch the train pull out of the station before heading for the stairs, deep in thought.

Chapter 2

September, 1972- Helmer Toro whistled to himself as he strolled through the door of his brother's bagel bakery and retail shop on 80th and Broadway. "H&H Midtown Bagels" had been a kosher staple of the Upper West Side when his brother Phillip decided to purchase it from its founders several years earlier.

The Upper West Side of Manhattan was a great location for a bagel shop, as New York's urban, Jewish professionals were all claiming stake for their families in this upscale, urban neighborhood.

H&H had really begun to develop a reputation for the quality of its kosher offerings in the neighborhood. People started to travel from different areas of the city just to get a taste of these hand-rolled, kettle-boiled, plank-baked gems. They were unlike any other bagels in the city. Some would say they were addictive. They were right. Allegations that this iconic symbol of the Jewish people was addictive was not a figurative notion. It was fact. You see, what the son of Puerto Rican sugar farmers came to understand very early in life, was that everything tastes better with sugar. Some experts have even argued that the addictive power of sugar exceeds that of the addictive power of drugs, including cocaine.

Helmer's cultural and religious separation from the traditional Jewish bagel makers of the Lower East Side provided him with the ability to look at the product as something other than one ideally suited for the breaking of the Sabbath. Helmer viewed it in culinary terms, and he was determined to make it better tasting. Sugar was his magic wand. As a result, his recipe became the foundation of what would become a Bagel Empire in a metropolis of sugar hungry New Yorkers.

As Helmer walked past the crew on this day, he was fixated on a single purpose. That purpose was to divest control of the bakery from his older brother. After all, it was Helmer that had created the 'secret' recipe for the bagels that were gaining popularity on the Upper West Side. It was Helmer that was in charge of the baking. Most significantly, it was Helmer that had gained the allegiance of the H&H employees. Helmer felt it was only natural that he ascend to his rightful place at the head of the H&H company.

Helmer enlisted the financial participation of his brother-in-law, Hector, who also worked in the bakery, for the venture. With Helmer, even in the 1970's, financial participation meant you put up all the money and took all the risk, while Helmer received all the upside of the venture.

Helmer, with Hector marching right behind him, walked down the basement stairs to the subterranean office that housed H&H's management.

"Morning, Helmer."

"Morning, Phillip. Can we talk?"

"Now, Helmer? We gotta get ready for the morning rush. Can't it wait?"

"No. We need to talk to you."

"We? Hector, what's up?"

"Listen, Phillip. We are taking over the bakery. We want you out. I raised $5,000 cash to buy you out. It's a fair offer."

"Helmer, are you out of your mind? Go back to work. The store is not for sale. Hector, what are you doing?"

"He's my partner. We are Helmer and Hector. H and H. You get it? Pretty good, huh?"

"Helmer, I don't have time for this nonsense. I bought this business with my savings. I brought you here after Vietnam when you had nothing. I gave you a job and a good living. Now you are going to try to muscle me out of my own place? Are you kidding me?"

With that, Helmer slowly shut the door to Phillip's office. The sounds of screaming interspersed with those of broken furniture could be heard upstairs in the retail store. The screaming was so intense that it resonated out onto Broadway. Most people couldn't make out what was being said in the frantic screams because they were in the form of a local

Spanish dialect. After two intense hours had passed, Helmer Toro, the ruthless negotiator, emerged as the new owner of H&H Bagels.

Chapter 3

November, 2010- Marcus sat in a holding cell, with a dozen or so inmates, awaiting his weekly discharge from the Eric M. Taylor Center (EMTC), or C76 as it was known. This was the area prisoners were moved to before they were released to the public. It was the final transfer point separating incarceration from freedom. Once they completed the steps here, former prisoners were put on a bus headed to Astoria and away from the dreaded island.

For Marcus, after his weekly Saturday processing, he was moved to what was known as a "house," which held 90 or so prisoners in a common holding area. This "house" was comprised of a series of metal-framed beds bolted to the floor, with paper-thin mattresses, creating the staunchest of barriers between flesh and metal. Each station had a small, clear, rectangular Rubbermaid container for approved personal belongings. There were no pillows allowed in EMTC, so most inmates rolled up left over sheets or hand towels as substitutes.

There was a large bathroom area in each "house," which contained several toilets and urinals, all completely visible to the prison guards as well as the entire "house" population. There were several shower heads, which were equally open to the guards and the prison population. These violations of individual privacy were forged in the spirit of dehumanizing the inmates, as much as in concerns for safety. Either way, for Marcus, being confined for less than 24 hours at a time, meant saving his showering for when he got home to his wife.

Each "house" had a small recreational room for use when earned by inmates and permitted by the Correction Officer on duty. The recreational room contained a small television which had numerous folding chairs lined up in front of it, movie theater style. While most of the chairs remained empty, they were "reserved" for various inmates. Sitting in a reserved seat, even in error, was akin to begging for a fight, so Marcus avoided the area completely. Some inmates played cards in the recreation area, while others wrote letters to family, using only the inserts of disposable pens removed from the plastic casing by guards, to avoid any potential creative weaponry.

Each "house" maintained a wall containing several phones across from the Guard Booth. Each prisoner was permitted to make two local calls of 6 minutes each every day. Phone calls were a valuable commodity on the island. Prisoners often, against Rikers policy, traded their phone minutes for commissary privileges and snacks smuggled in from the cafeteria. Marcus used his allotted time to call his wife and family to assure them he was safe.

The demographic of the "house," like Rikers itself, was over 95% Blacks and Hispanics. This ratio held true for the Corrections Officers, as well as the inmates. While Marcus was not normally conscious of race, it was hard not to notice being such a distinct minority in the city prison system. As a white "Weekend Warrior" – a prisoner that came and left each weekend – it was hard for him to achieve the goal of simply blending into the prison population.

While his minority status didn't make him feel any more vulnerable than simply being locked in such a violent penal colony, what was of concern to him was the stark gang-related divide between Blacks and Hispanics that existed in the prison, and in each "house." Marcus had no place on either side of the battle, but early on it was apparent to him that he needed to choose a side, and choose wisely, in order to survive the weekends.

While he didn't exactly choose sides, the circumstances of his incarceration placed him under the protection of the Hispanics. When Marcus was processed upon his entry to EMTC, his 6'2, 240lb frame was too large for any of the green Rikers jumpsuits that were available from laundry services, so he was issued a brand new one, right out of the package. While Marcus didn't think too much about his green jumper, the newness of it attracted the attention of many of the prisoners, perhaps believing his color and race had something to do with his receiving the benefit.

On Marcus' first visit to the urinal, a very sizable, African-American inmate came up behind him and placed his arm on Marcus' shoulder. "You one of those weekend warriors, right?" the man inquired.

Marcus knew this was not a good start to the relationship. "Yes," he said as he attempted to pass the man.

"Not so quick, son," the man said, blocking his way. "The way I see it, you are only here on the weekends. I got 10 months left. I need that new jumper more than you. Switch with me."

"Excuse me?" Marcus said, really not yet processing what was going on.

"You heard me. You give me your jumper and I'll give you mine. Let's go."

"I can't do that," Marcus insisted. "I don't want any trouble."

"No trouble, cupcake, just do what I tell you and no trouble at all."

Marcus thought for a second, completely unsure of what to do. He knew that giving up the jumpsuit wouldn't get him in trouble, but it would be a sign of weakness that would lead to more and more demands from this inmate and his cohorts. To fight, on the other hand, would have landed him in solitary confinement and risked a revocation of his lenient sentence. He was paralyzed with indecision.

"He is with me," a voice said. "So back the fuck off." It was Helmer Toro, the well-known and respected New York City Bagel Tycoon, and weekend warrior himself, serving time for New York State tax evasion. Marcus and Toro had struck up a friendship due to the similarity of their circumstances. What Marcus didn't know was that Toro was Puerto Rican; he looked more German, actually. More importantly, Toro was under the protection of one of the three major Hispanic gangs in New York that were entrenched in the prison system.

Upon Toro's entrance and command, the menacing inmate turned, and, without a word, exited the bathroom area.

"Thank you," Marcus muttered.

"No thanks needed. We warriors gotta look out for each other. Come here, kid. We got a bunk picked out for you."

"You know me?" Marcus asked.

"Sure, kid. I read all about your case in the paper. We follow all the weekend warriors. Let me introduce you to the boys."

With that, Helmer proceeded to introduce the half a dozen or so men that he had created an oasis within this maximum-security facility. All the men were cordial and inviting, and all seemed to acknowledge Toro as the leader of the pack.

"Sit down, kid. Step into my office."

Toro motioned for Marcus to sit next to him on the bunk Helmer had selected for himself.

"You know who I am?"

"I am not sure I understand the question."

"H&H. That's me. I am that guy.'

"Oh," said Marcus, still not really sure what that meant, or what exactly H&H was. "What are you in for, Helmer?"

"A little tax mix-up. I made a deal for weekends instead of having to repay the money. I got the better end of the deal, I think." He snickered.

"You're a lawyer, right?"

"Not anymore."

"Yeah, but I mean by training."

"Yes."

"Okay. I need your advice."

Toro and Marcus then proceeded to spend the next several hours talking generally about commercial real estate and finance. Helmer was outlining a series of complex cross-collateralized, commercial mortgage transactions that were encumbering some of his properties, and looking for ideas on how to void the agreements. He was looking to avoid making payments without losing the properties in foreclosure. For Marcus, this was a breath of fresh air. Feeling secure and being able to talk comfortably about intellectual areas that he was familiar with helped him to pass the time and forget that he was confined to the largest, and one of the most brutal, penal colonies in the world. He asked Helmer a series of questions as they talked over some scenarios.

What Marcus didn't realize was that this wasn't just a friendly conversation between two inmates. It was a job interview.

"I could use a guy like you. Come work for me. You can start right away."

"Excuse me?" Marcus was stunned. Of all of the things he expected to come from his time at Rikers, a job offer wasn't one of them.

"Helmer, I don't have any food experience. I don't know anything about bagels."

"That's okay."

"I have never been directly involved in manufacturing either."

"Fine, Fine, Fine. Kid, I want you for the office. I have a lot going on and I could use a guy with your skills and your brains."

"Helmer, I am really flattered but you don't even know me. You know I am not licensed to practice law anymore?"

"Yeah, yeah, yeah. I know. There is still a lot to do. Is that a yes?"

"Yes, sure."

"Great. Report Monday morning to 80th and Broadway. That's the office. The girls will set you up in the system. Welcome aboard."

Chapter 4

The city bus came to a halt, seemingly in the middle of nowhere, to let the newly released prisoners off of the island. Marcus stepped off the bus and looked around for his wife's car, which he saw idling across the street. He crossed in front of the bus and headed towards her Volkswagen Jetta. She leaned over to open the passenger side door and let him in.

"Baby," she said.

"Hi, honey," he said as he leaned in to give her a kiss.

"Was it horrible?"

"You are never gonna believe what happened."

He went on to relay the entire story with some incredulity, even though he had experienced it firsthand. Besides his shock and confusion, he confided in his wife that he wasn't even sure who Helmer Toro or H&H Bagels was.

"Isn't that where Kramer worked?"

"Kramer who?"

"From ***Seinfeld***. Don't you remember the episode where Kramer went to work at a bagel store. I am pretty sure that was H&H."

Marcus' feverish midnight inquiries would reveal that she was in fact correct. During the early 1990's, H&H Bagels was in a bit of financial decline. After twenty years of Helmer Toro's ownership, the store's antiquated appearance, high prices, limited product offering, poor service, and a "cash only" policy seemed to have contributed to the brand losing some of its luster and relevance. In fact, much of its business was now comprised solely of local families that had grown up on the product, as opposed to new prospects from around the city and curiosity seekers.

By contrast, ***Seinfeld*** was NBC's top rated television show during the 1990's. Its distinctly New York style and comedic timing made it a television sensation. In 1996, almost 40 million viewers tuned in to watch Jerry Seinfeld and the ensemble cast of this groundbreaking show "about nothing."

Episode 166 of ***Seinfeld***, "The Strike," centered on Cosmo Kramer's return to work to H&H Bagels, his previously unmentioned employer, after a 12-year labor strike. The bagel company, its products, logo, and slogan were all prominently featured throughout the prime-time episode. It was this comedic celebrity endorsement that instantly propelled H&H Bagels from local New York City business to international phenomena. Bagel lovers and television junkies throughout the United States, across Europe, and from as far away as Taiwan and South Korea all insisted they had to have the bagel that was featured in their beloved sitcom. They were willing to pay substantial prices to have these bagels frozen and shipped to them for bake off and sale in their regional markets.

H&H Bagels, fueled by the show's enormous popularity, re-emerged as a financial and manufacturing dynamo. The television tie-in generated a wholesale demand that necessitated production of almost 100,000 bagels a day in order to meet the interest of a bagel hungry public. The finest hotels, gourmet delicatessens, and Kosher distributors all over the world had to have their H&H Bagels in order to satisfy their customers and guests.

It wasn't just the product itself that businesses and consumers all over the world were interested in. It was also the brand that they wanted to be associated with. Everyone wanted to be able to share the beloved brand that was featured on ***Seinfeld***. Many New Yorkers proudly boasted of having been loyal customers before the television revival. The store's trademarked slogan *"Like No Other Bagels in the World,"* instantly became a recognizable and valuable piece of intellectual property.

As is common practice in the entertainment industry, many producers are only willing to bet on a sure thing. This conservative "imitation is the sincerest form of flattery" philosophy lead to an army of other television programs, movies, and magazine articles on subjects from food to business, to feature what had now become the most beloved bagel product in the history of the world. These appearances included movies like Tom Hanks' ***You've Got Mail,*** Woody Allen's ***Manhattan Murder Mystery,*** and wildly popular television shows like ***Friends, The Office, Saturday Night Live, Entourage,*** and ***Sex in the City***. Each appearance acted as an international booster shot of fame and brand recognition for this once ethnic only product line reserved for Jewish New York City dwellers.

For Helmer Toro, the once impoverished son of a sugar cane farmer, all of this focus and attention not only propelled his business financially, but it thrust him into the spotlight as one of New York's new quasi-celebrities. The man who had once spent his mornings kneading, rolling, and twisting five ounces of high gluten dough into a New York City bagel, with its dark crusty exterior and light chewy interior, found himself spending his evenings in the company of Manhattan's elite. Helmer's companions included celebrities like Alec Baldwin and Jerry Seinfeld, musicians like

Barbara Streisand, politicians like Brooklyn Borough President Marty Markowitz, and even U.S. President Bill Clinton, an admitted H&H lover.

Among those elite Manhattan socialites was Dr. Amy Dukoff, the renowned Manhattan Endodontist of Jewish descent and significant financial means. Dr. Dukoff, a woman much more accustomed to traveling in elite circles than Toro, was an unlikely candidate to become the wife of this bagel maven. Yet that is exactly what happened. This union might have been the truest measure that Helmer Toro had arrived socially.

"So with all this fame, celebrity, and success, how did Helmer Toro end up spending 50 weekends on Rikers Island?" Marcus said to himself.

Marcus found himself unable to cease his investigation into the history of Helmer Toro and the H&H Empire, regardless of the lateness of the hour. He did not want to walk into his new position on the following day without discovering everything he could about the place he was planning on calling home for the foreseeable future. He continued to scroll through the mass of articles on the history of the company. His searches lead him to a slew of articles about the reason for Helmer's incarceration. The headlines from papers like the **NY Times** read, *"Helmer Toro, H&H Bagels Owner, Admits Cheating On Taxes,"* **The NY Daily News,** *"Bagel Man Gone Bad or Schmear Campaign? H&H Bagel owner Helmer Toro Charged with Tax Fraud,"* and **The NY Post**, *"H&H Bagel Man may Hand Over Lots of Dough in Tax Cheat Case."*

The essence of all of the articles was the same. While each one touched on various aspects of the history and fame of the bagel giant, they all talked about Toro's indictment and conviction for failing to pay withholding taxes for his hundreds of employees. The stories all talked about Robert Morgenthau, the Manhattan District Attorney, looking to make an example of Toro for other members of the food industry. This was the type of prosecution that Marcus found distasteful.

“Despite any wrongdoing on Toro’s part, prosecutions should be for the crimes committed, not to set an example,” Marcus thought to himself. Perhaps, it hit a little too close to home for him regarding his own legal troubles.

He thought long and hard about whether anything he read in the articles made him reconsider the opportunity he was about to embark on. Not really. It was no secret that Helmer Toro was a convicted felon. He did meet Helmer on Rikers Island, after all. Toro was forthcoming that his conviction was for tax evasion, and that his deal included 50 weekends of jail time, plus some restitution. All true by every account.

“A lot of people cheat on their taxes,” he thought. “That doesn’t make him a bad guy.”

The one underlying issue that the articles discussed, which Helmer never mentioned, involved the formation of a series of corporate entities to obfuscate the government’s ability to figure out the scheme and to link it to him. It seemed like this aspect was a bit more calculated than a mere failure to pay withholding taxes, but maybe it was nothing. He was too tired to really consider it tonight. Tomorrow would be another day.

Chapter 5

As Marcus sat on the westbound Bayside express line of the Long Island Railroad, his cell phone rang. He looked down at the display and saw a phone number he didn't recognize. Despite that, he answered.

"Hello. Marcus?"

"Hello," he replied cautiously, still not recognizing the voice.

"It's me, Helmer. I need you to come to my apartment before we go to the office. We have something important to take care of. It's 70th and Broadway, The Coronado. I will tell the doorman to let you up."

"Okay. See you soon."

The Coronado, the city residence of Helmer and Amy Toro, was a distinctive 22 story corner brick building built in 1989. "People find the two large cast stone gargoyles that flank the entranceway on 70th Street one of its memorable features. This full service condo, with 24-hour doorman and 24-hour concierge, has a huge 12,000 square foot amenity floor with an inviting children's playroom complete with its own tree house visible from the street. There is a billiard room with Ping-Pong tables, a resident's lounge with full kitchen and a fabulous on site gym, health club and sauna. It is conveniently located in Lincoln Square, close to Central Park, Lincoln Center, excellent shopping and restaurants and only 2 blocks to the new 72nd Street subway station and express and local IRT lines." (Coronado Sales Flyer)

Marcus was impressed by the majesty of the building and its classical Upper West Side, New York City elegance. This was a place where professional, upper class people resided in New York. The residents of The Coronado were the kind of people that only left Manhattan to go on vacation, or to visit their summer homes in the Hamptons. It was a stark contrast to the conditions Helmer was subjected to during his weekend stints at Rikers.

As Marcus approached the front door he could hear what sounded like screaming from inside the apartment housing the Toro family. It sounded like a very serious argument was ensuing, especially for 7AM in the morning. As he stood outside the doorway he hesitated for a moment, not sure whether it was better to come back after the screaming had ceased. While he wanted to be respectful, he found himself concerned about being late for his first day of work. He hoped that a knock on the door might be a welcome surprise for the combatants inside the luxury apartment unit.

Marcus rang the doorbell, which at first did little to quell the screaming inside. Then, he heard a female voice bark out an order.

"Get the door, Helmer."

As Marcus stood in the hall he sensed the presence of a person on the opposite side of the closed door. He then heard the sound of a chain being unlatched, a deadbolt being opened, and a doorknob being turned as the door opened revealing his new employer. Helmer was standing before him in his underwear, seemingly unconcerned that just anybody could be on the other side of the door. Marcus instinctively looked away in embarrassment.

"I can come back."

"No, no, no. Come in. Sit down," he said, pointing to the dining room table. Literally every inch of the long table, but for a small section where a laptop was positioned, was covered with high stacks of legal papers.

Standing next to the table was a pale, petite woman that appeared to be readying herself to walk out the door. She had a briefcase and overcoat in hand, and she wore a brimmed hat that matched her overcoat. She was considerably younger than Helmer, and Marcus suspected she was Helmer's wife, Amy, and the source of all of the screaming.

"You're the lawyer?"

"No ma'am. I am not a lawyer anymore. Nice to meet you. I am Marcus."

Amy looked at Marcus but not respond to his introduction.

"Helmer, I tell you, I am going to the FBI. This is intimidation and blackmail and I am having everybody arrested. Bob Benjamin. Jay Friedrich. Jorge DelGado. Do you hear me, Helmer? Everyone is going to jail. It's RICO! I tell you, RICO! Do you understand, Helmer?" She was screaming at this point and she, clearly, had no concern that a stranger was in their presence.

"Stop, Amy. You are going to be late."

She looked down at her watch and realized that it was, indeed, late. With that, on a dime, she transformed from a volatile, impassioned orator to Dr. Amy Dukoff Toro. She walked over and kissed Helmer quickly on the lips and headed for the door, as if no altercation had been previously occurred.

"Have a good day, Helmer." She was off.

Helmer then proceeded, in his underwear, to make himself a single fried egg, over medium, with buttered white toast, and a cup of espresso style Café Bustelo coffee. While he prepared his breakfast, he said nothing. He said nothing about Amy's tirade. Nothing about the job. Nothing at all. He was silent.

He then sat at the dining room table and replaced the laptop with his breakfast plate. He proceeded to, silently, eat and read the newspaper. He offered Marcus nothing, which was fine by him. He just found it odd. The odd nature of this entire initial encounter had Marcus feeling a little uneasy about his decision to join forces with this man that he really knew nothing about.

This breakfast ritual, Marcus would learn, went on every day. It was more of a religious experience than a breakfast. Helmer would not leave his apartment, no matter the circumstances, until he made himself this exact breakfast.

After Helmer finished eating and got dressed, he turned to Marcus and spoke for the first time in some while.

"You ready to get some work done?"

"Absolutely."

Helmer then led him out of the apartment building and onto to 70th Street. He offered no instructions, but Marcus followed him as he walked briskly along the street. Marcus wondered where they were headed with such a sense of purpose. Finally, they stopped in front of two parked cars. One was a large tan Chevy Suburban. The second was a small, black, Mini-Cooper. Neither vehicle appeared to be in good shape, nor was, particularly, new. Helmer handed him the keys to the Mini-Cooper.

"Start up the engine and sit in the driver's seat until the meter maid passes. I will be in the Suburban."

"Excuse me?"

"This is a no parking zone until 10AM. We need to sit here until she passes and pretend we are loading or unloading or we will get a parking ticket."

Marcus was completely confused. Was this some sort of joke, or a test? Was he hired to sit for one hour, inside an idling car, to help his tycoon employer avoid a parking ticket?

Apparently, the answer to that question was yes. During the period of his employment with H&H, Marcus would report first to Helmer's apartment to engage in this daily ritual of "beat the meter maid" before doing any other work. This was Helmer's top priority. He made all of his appointments around this schedule. Sometimes he even held meetings in his car rather than pay for parking. Later on, when Marcus was more comfortable speaking to Helmer, he asked him why he didn't simply park the vehicles in the garage at The Coronado. They offered parking and most of the residents didn't own cars, so there was always an open spot.

"It costs $200 a month for a spot at The Coronado. It's a rip-off."

"You do realize that if you calculated the hours you are paying for me to sit and babysit your car, that it comes out to a lot more than $200 a month?"

"Yeah, yeah, yeah. It's okay."

As Marcus sat behind the wheel of the idling Mini-Cooper, listening to the radio and checking his messages, all the while keeping a keen eye out for the City's parking attendant, he thought to himself, "What has happened to my life?"

Chapter 6

Once the morning car ritual was completed, Helmer knocked on the window of the Mini-Cooper and instructed Marcus to slide over into the passenger seat.

"Wanna see the production facilities?"

"I would love to." Marcus was excited to be able to visit the heart of all of the excitement and fanfare.

"First Stop, Secaucus, New Jersey."

"New Jersey?" Marcus asked.

"Yeah, yeah, yeah. Secaucus, that's where the bagels are made".

"They are made in New Jersey? But isn't part of the appeal that you are a genuine, New York City Bagel? Isn't that what you advertise?"

Helmer put his finger in front of his own mouth and hunched forward with a slightly sinister look on his face.

"Shhh. Nobody really cares about that anymore. They just love the brand. They can't really tell the difference."

"Really?" Marcus argued. "I have been doing a lot of reading on this subject over the last couple of days and everything I read says that New York City water has the best balance of minerals and PH alkalinity. The articles also talked about the air components as all factoring in to why everyone loves New York City bagels and pizza. The articles seemed to say that even when people take the exact same recipes and try to duplicate them outside of New York, the difference is noticeable."

Helmer just shrugged and didn't respond. Marcus thought he must have stumbled upon something, because he remembered reading comments from reviewers on food websites remarking that the quality of the product had noticeably diminished in recent years. The reviewers didn't know the reason, or at least they didn't mention it. But Marcus wondered if it wasn't the relocation to New Jersey that factored into this deterioration in quality.

35 UPS Drive was a mammoth, 75,000 square foot, one-story building in Secaucus, New Jersey. The property was the most land locked of four properties, positioned in a cluster. The other three properties were owned by the shipping giant United Parcel Service, hence the name of the street. Helmer later bragged to Marcus how he had frustrated UPS' effort to obtain this parcel. He hoped to eventually parlay their desire to close off access to the street into a sizable buy-out.

"Here we are."

Helmer proceeded to provide a tour of this mammoth facility, which was the centerpiece of H&H Bagels' wholesale production. Marcus was amazed that of the 75,0000 square feet of space, less than 20% of the floor plan was allocated towards any type of bagel production or food storage. The remainder was filled with what appeared to be nothing more than junk. It looked more like a scrap-metal warehouse than a food manufacturing facility.

As Helmer lead him into the production area, Marcus could see the scurrying of workers, all wearing tan shirts and hats that bore the familiar H&H logo: a little brown shopping bag and the phrase, *"Like No Other Bagel in the World."* As Helmer marched past clusters of workers Marcus could hear them calling out "El Jefe." While Marcus' Spanish wasn't very good, he did recognize that this was Spanish for "Chief." He also recalled that this was one of the common nicknames for Cuba's communist dictator, Fidel Castro.

This core of overwhelmingly Hispanic workers looked at Helmer with great affinity. They viewed him, with his Tourneau watch and his family ski trips to Vail, Colorado, as a symbol of the achievement of the American Dream. Despite his recent misfortune, he was who they wanted to be some day. They trusted him and he knew it.

"Helmer, can you walk me through the process since I have no idea of what's going on."

"Sure, sure, sure." This request seemed to excite Helmer in a way Marcus hadn't experienced yet. He seemed to achieve a focus that evidenced that, at his core, he loved bagels. His reaction was pure.

Helmer led him to a mixing area where there were two huge metal cylinders that were fully closed and spinning quickly. These were Peerless Horizontal Mixers. Peerless were the most highly regarded mixers in the bagel business, Helmer explained.

"Each of these mixers holds 900lbs of dough. Once the machine is done mixing the dough, these workers cut it into chunks and feed into the Thompson bagel former."

The Thompson Bagel machine was invented in 1963 by Daniel Thompson as a way to replace hand rollers in the bagel process. This machine revolutionized the bagel business by allowing companies like Lender's Bagels to mass-produce bagels for the wholesale market. The major critics of the machine suggested that it also compromised the quality of the finished product. The critics were correct, Marcus surmised.

Helmer then led Marcus to the area where a large mechanical device on the machine was feeding large chunks of dough into one end and spitting out the familiar, circular bagels on the other end. Women with wooden boards were quickly placing the rolled dough onto the boards in rows, and loading them onto rolling racks. Marcus couldn't help but think about the famous "I Love Lucy" episode where Lucy and Ethel got jobs on a chocolate factory assembly line, and couldn't keep up with the speed of production.

"Those racks go in the cooling box for overnight cooling and retarding."

Rolled bagels sitting overnight in a cool space is part of the secret of their taste. Bagel dough contains live yeast. As the yeast breaks down the starches in the dough, natural sugar is created through the fermentation process. This is where the flavor comes from. Most table breads are baked within a short time after the dough is mixed, not leaving sufficient time for a rich flavor to develop. With bagels, however, they need to sit for 12-18 hours after mixing, which creates the flavor.

Historically, Sabbath observers, before the start of the Sabbath, rolled bagels on the Friday before sunset. When the Sabbath ended on Saturday night at sunset the bagels simply needed to be baked and eaten to break the fast of the Sabbath. This is part of the reason why they are so connected to the Jewish faith.

Marcus was fascinated by the culinary tour of this historic facility for a product he had enjoyed his whole life but, really, knew nothing about. He realized that he had never really thought about the process that went into making bagels, or their cultural significance. He would never look at a bagel the same way again.

Marcus and Helmer then moved on to an area where workers were pulling racks out of the retarder and moving them towards a long conveyor belt, which had a giant caldron of boiling water in front of it.

"Those are the bagels that were rolled yesterday. They let them get acclimated to room temperature and then they feed them into the kettle."

"Kettle?"

"Yes, they bagels are boiled for 1-2 minutes to seal in the flavor and create the luster you see. This is part of the age-old secret of good bagels. If they sink when you drop them in the cauldron they are not ready to be baked yet. The bagels themselves tell you when they are ready. How cool is that?"

Marcus watched as workers dumped the bagels from the boards into the kettle, and they floated to the top. As they floated around the murky water, looking like inner tubes on a lagoon, workers would scoop them up with a giant ladle and place them on a metal conveyor. This metal conveyor led them into a long, modern tunnel oven, where they were baked without ever being touched by human hands. The tunnel oven replaced the old fashion, fired, rotating deck oven, which had workers baking bagels on wooden planks and turning them by hand. This was another modern development that Marcus had read contributed to the disintegration of the quality of a modern bagel.

"After the bagels are baked they automatically feed down the assembly line cooling tower to the packaging area where they are packed and frozen for shipment around the world, even as far away as China," Helmer said proudly.

"Helmer, this is really amazing."

"Yeah, yeah, yeah," he said.

Chapter 7

Helmer signaled to Marcus to follow him to a remote part of the facility, somewhat removed from the area where all the buzz of the workers was taking place. Helmer guided him down and dark path and around a steep corner. Helmer picked up the pace as he approached the place where he planned to unveil something that's significance would not be apparent to Marcus at first. As Marcus rounded the corner, he saw a gigantic, cavernous, excavated hole. A hole that looked like it might have been part of construction at one time but now was just a hole. The hole trumped any other area of the facility in size, including where the bagels were being produced.

"Well, what do you think?"

Marcus wasn't sure what to make of the question, especially because Helmer seemed so excited by what lie before them.

"What is it?"

"It's the future, kid."

"The future? I don't understand."

"This is the reason I bought this building."

"A giant, dirt floor hole?"

Helmer laughed. As he stared into the distance, at the center of the vast cavern, he seemed to drift off into a trance-like state, like he was lost in a dream. He had the look of a man possessed. He reminded Marcus of the diabolical villain, Goldfinger, from the 1964 James Bond classic film.

"This is what will make H&H the most successful bagel company in the history of world."

"Explain, please."

"This 'dirt floor hole,' as you call it, is the foundation of an 800 pallet, frozen bagel freezer. Once this is completed it will give me the ability to store and distribute frozen bagels around the world without having to pay storage costs or packing fees to any third parties. In fact, other companies will come here to store their products for us to do their distribution, and pay us for those services and storage charges."

A pallet is the way in which large, frozen bagel orders are packed for shipment. A standard U.S. pallet is 40"x48" in length and, about, 6 feet tall. The weight can vary depending on the product type; for bagels the weight was about 1000lbs. For H&H Bagels, a pallet was comprised of approximately 300 dozen bagels for domestic and international shipment. Helmer's design called for the storage of almost half a million bagels at a time for global domination of the frozen bagel markct.

There was just one problem with Helmer's plan: the cost. As Marcus would learn, Helmer managed to use other people's money to fund all of his projects. Sometimes those funds came from banks, sometimes from private individuals, and sometimes from places like employees' withholding taxes. Helmer had borrowed considerable money to buy 35 UPS Drive, and had cross-collateralized it with all the equity on his building on West 46th Street in Manhattan. This was the lending scenario

Helmer had run buy Marcus during their initial "interview" on Rikers. These were the loans that Helmer was trying so desperately to void, and now Marcus was starting to understand why.

Helmer was more than $3 million dollars into the construction of the freezer, but less than half way completed on the project when New York State indicted him for failing to remit the withholding taxes he had taken from the 120 employees listed on his payroll. Once he was a convicted felon, all of his lending sources ceased doing business with him. His personal and business credit completely dried up. No one would lend Helmer Toro a dime. Since the foundation of Helmer's debt service payments relied not on the funds from bagel production, but from income and cost savings from this "freezer of the future," the failure to be able to fund the completion of the freezer construction was, in and of itself, the nail in the H&H coffin.

"Finishing this freezer is our top priority, kid. Nothing else is more important."

Marcus looked over at Helmer and he could see a look that he would see many times in Helmer over the course of his employment. This was the look of a man fixated on achieving his personal goals at anyone's cost and expense.

Marcus was a quick study. He was only on the job for one day, but he was already starting to put the pieces of the puzzle together. This company, and this man, had a lot of serious and complex issues to be dealt with.

"This job may not be a long term career path after all," he thought.

Chapter 8

As Helmer and Marcus approached the front of the historic retail store on 80th and Broadway, Helmer slowed the Mini-Cooper in front of a pile of garbage that was blocking the street. He honked the horn and two seemingly homeless men, that had appeared to be sleeping against the side of the building, jumped to attention and transferred all of the garbage onto the sidewalk to allow him to park, easily, in front of the store. Marcus laughed to himself.

"This guy has an angle for everything," he thought.

"Gracias, Amigos," he said as he jumped out, tipped the brim of his hat to the two street urchins, and handed them each a single dollar bill.

"Cheapest parking in the City," he snickered.

Out of the corner of Marcus' eye he saw a small, inconspicuous sign in the window of the store that read, "Not affiliated with H&H Midtown East." He didn't need to ask Helmer about this sign because he had read about it on the train ride in earlier that day. It seemed that Helmer Toro had made several attempts in the years after his acquisition of the 80th Street store to expand the business. One such attempt was the opening of a midtown store, which he cleverly called H&H Midtown East because of its location. In the 1980's, when the business was previously on the verge of closing, Helmer filed for Federal Bankruptcy Protection and the Federal Court Judge split the assets of the business as part of the case. Helmer retained the original location, and a bidder at an auction took the midtown location, keeping the H&H Midtown East title.

In the 1990's, once H&H started becoming popular again, Helmer filed a Federal Trademark Infringement lawsuit to compel the midtown store to stop using his famous brand name. The case claimed "likelihood of confusion" on the part of the public over the affiliation of the two independent businesses. While Helmer was probably legally correct, the Judge ruled that, in part, due to Helmer's decade long delay in bringing the suit, the two stores could keep their names, subject to posting a disclaimer informing the public that they were not under the same ownership.

Marcus took a deep breath as he crossed the threshold of the most famous bagel store in the world. As he walked in he was a little surprised. He wasn't sure what to expect but a dark, dingy, empty bagel store was definitely not what he anticipated. There was no place to sit. The décor looked like it hadn't been renovated or cleaned since Toro took over the place in the early 1970's. Clear plexiglass bins were filled with the traditional bagel varieties: Plain, Everything, Sesame, Poppy, Cinnamon Raisin, Whole Wheat, and so on. Marcus noticed a large sign over the register that read "CASH ONLY" and another sign that said bagels sold for $1.40 apiece.

"Wow, that is insane." On Long Island, where Marcus grew up, you could get a fresh bagel almost anywhere for $0.85.

There were two workers visible. One was a Hispanic woman, who was sitting at the cash register and appeared to be falling asleep. The second employee, a man, was stationed at an old fashioned, rotating deck bagel oven. He was flipping bagels from wooden boards onto the clay shelving of the oven, by hand. This, unlike the way the bagels were being made in the New Jersey facility, was the traditional way to bake bagels. This made sense to Marcus because it was this location's bagels that were being delivered to some of the finest establishments in New York City, like Helmer's neighbor, Zabar's, and Barney Greengrass. Their discerning customers would certainly know the difference between a traditional bagel and the ones being made in New Jersey. It was then that Marcus realized that Helmer was using these high profile accounts, and his brand recognition, to garner sales interest outside of New York City. However, since the cost of making traditional bagels is very high, and very labor intensive, he would fill these large orders with the inferior, mass-produced version of his product with the expectation that the end user would never know the difference. It was only "signature" accounts that received the traditional H&H Bagels.

Helmer walked quickly towards a door at the rear of the retail store. He stopped only briefly to pull a plain bagel from the basket and squeeze it, then smell it, and toss it back without saying a word.

The rear door lead down a flight of stairs to the subterranean offices that housed the corporate headquarters of H&H Bagels. As Helmer proceeded to introduce Marcus to everyone, Marcus noticed that everyone spoke almost exclusively Spanish. Like the production workers, the office staff also all referred to Toro by the title, "El Jefe."

There were so many people working in this office complex that Marcus knew it would be awhile before he figured out who everybody was and what their functions were.

Two people in particular stood out in that initial introduction, however. The first was the kindly Korean War veteran named Norman

Levy, who Marcus learned was the National Sales Manager. Norman, it turned out, was a beloved legend of the bagel business. He was known and trusted by wholesale accounts around the world. Norman's gentle demeanor, good humor, and ethnic profile made him an ideal face for the sales department. He was extremely generous in sharing with Marcus his knowledge of the industry and H&H.

The second was Brian Confino, in house counsel. Brian was an extremely young, soft-spoken man. As Marcus walked in, he was reading a document and running his fingers through his hair. He seemed very anxious. He lacked the confident demeanor of most of the lawyers that Marcus had ever encountered. His desk was positioned next to Helmer's in an office suitable for one person but housed three. Brian and Helmer's desk, like Helmer's dining room table, had every inch of their surface covered with stacks and stacks of legal documents.

"Brian, this is Marcus. He is one of my fellow weekend warriors. He is gonna be helping us out." Brian immediately got a look of relief on his face as he stood up to say hello and shake Marcus' hand.

Marcus was starting to understand why Helmer was so interested in him coming aboard, despite his inexperience in the food industry. He understood, now, what he would be spending his time focusing on.

Chapter 9

Marcus sat at his kitchen table studying the paperwork that attorney Brian Confino had provided him in order to familiarize himself with the corporate entities that came under the umbrella of the organization that was H&H Bagels. While it was common for corporations to operate their businesses using multiple legal entities in order to shield themselves from liability, Marcus guessed the structure of the H&H family of businesses was unmatched in the modern annals of business. Marcus couldn't help but recall that most of the stories about Toro's withholding tax issues involved allegations of the use of shell companies.

H&H Legal Entities

The First Toro Family Limited Partnership

The Second Toro Family Limited Partnership

The Third Toro Family Limited Partnership

The Fourth Toro Family Limited Partnership

The Fifth Toro Family Limited Partnership

The Sixth Toro Family Limited Partnership

The Seventh Toro Family Limited Partnership

The Eighth Toro Family Limited Partnership

Manhattan West Side Limited Partnership

35 Real Estate LP

Garden Operation Realty LP

Jersey Employee Services Corp.

XYZ III Inc.

VUT VI Inc.

PQR VII Inc.

QRS II Inc.

TUV V Inc.

ZXY I Inc.

West Side Storage Inc.

Riverway Management Inc.

West Mill Limited Partnership

Wingate Limited Partnership

H&H Properties

2239 Broadway, NY, NY

639 West 46th Street, NY, NY

35 UPS Drive, Secaucus, NJ

Marcus spent the next few days familiarizing himself with the entities and properties comprising H&H and the various ways that they were interconnected. He also read a series of formation documents and Limited Partnership Agreements that all allocated 95% ownership not to Helmer Toro, but to Amy Toro, his wife. The remaining 5% was owned by Helmer, as General Partner, conferring all of the decision making power on him, but only 5% of the liability. Behind the mask of this affable, uncomfortable, quirky man, there was a ruthless businessman, Marcus conjectured.

Corporations, contracts, and pre-nuptial agreements all have one thing in common. When things are good, no one bothers to care what they say. But, when things go bad, everyone scrambles to see what they can hang their hat on for the purposes of initiating, or defending lawsuits. This was no less true in the world of H&H.

In addition to all of these formation documents, Marcus had a stack of lawsuits and legal claims to familiarize himself with. These included lawsuits where one or more of the H&H entities or owners individually were defending against the claims of:

The IRS

Manhattan District Attorney's Office

NYS Department of Taxation & Finance

New Jersey Tax Department

Robert Benjamin

DLC Holdings

DRA Asia

Friedland Properties

National Labor Relations Board

Hudson Energy

Griffin Cosmo

Benjamin Silverman

Marilyn Dukoff

Wilenta Feed & Carting

Archer Daniels Midland (ADM)

to name just a few that Marcus was getting caught up on.

In addition to the well-publicized withholding tax problems Helmer Toro was facing, Marcus poured through foreclosure documents for the New Jersey and West Side properties owned by H&H, an eviction proceeding for the property on 80th Street, a series of tax claims on the State and Federal level against all of the entities, labor complaints, and the very complex leasehold litigation initiated by long-time Helmer Toro business partner, Robert Benjamin. Marcus felt like becoming familiar with H&H and its structure and problems read like a veritable course on business law. The issues touched on corporations, partnerships, foreclosures, criminal law, mortgages, commercial finance, leases, landlord and tenant law, tax law, contract law, intellectual property law, and bankruptcy. "This is uncanny," Marcus thought to himself. What he found most intriguing, more interesting than any other aspect of this legal complexity and confusion, was that it was all about BAGELS.

Chapter 10

Marcus sat at Helmer's dining room table reading an IRS decision ruling that "All of the entities of H&H Bagels were alter-egos of Helmer Toro for tax purposes and vice-versa," and therefore, all taxes due and owing against Helmer individually or any one of the entities could be levied against them all. The basis for the decision was the IRS' determination that the assets of the individual entities were not properly segregated, as required by law, but were commingled, destroying any protections normally afforded corporations and their shareholders. As Marcus was looking for a way to understand the impact on the business, his phone rang. It was the manager of the 46th Street location.

"Marcus, is Helmer with you?"

"Yes, why?"

"You better tell him the State is here and they are padlocking the place."

"What? Why? What is going on?"

"They are saying Helmer broke his payment arrangement on sales taxes and they are seizing everything."

"How much are we behind?"

"$8,000.00"

"Holy, cow! Hold on." With that, he muted the phone and explained to Helmer what was going on. Helmer seemed unconcerned by the news.

"Okay, tell him to let them know we will be right there. Not to take anything. See if they will take less money, too."

"Helmer says we are on our way. Let me speak to the lead enforcement officer."

"This is Agent Simmons. With whom am I speaking?"

"This is Marcus from the corporate office. I am with Helmer Toro and we are on our way to the store to resolve this matter. We may be a little short. What is the minimum we can bring and keep the store open?"

“You tell Toro I am tired of these games. We are proceeding with the lock up. It may take a while. If he gets here with the $8,000.00 before we are done, in good funds, I will have no choice but to release the property, but not a penny less.”

Marcus relayed the conversation to Helmer who seemed completely unfazed.

“Okay, I guess we will pay it all.”

With that he went back to making his eggs, toast, and Café Bustelo. Not even a real emergency could stop the consumption of his morning meal. Marcus had never met anyone like Helmer before.

After finishing getting dressed, Helmer went into the top drawer of his dresser, where he kept his clean socks, and pulled out a large wad of bills. They were rolled into a cylinder and had a thick rubber band around them. It must have been, at least, $10,000.00.

“Let’s go, kid. We should make it just in time.”

639 West 46th Street was a two story, 25,000 square foot building located in the Hell's Kitchen section of Manhattan. It was directly across from the Intrepid Air and Space Museum, and had been purchased by Helmer Toro, with the assistance of Amy's parents, some years earlier. It had housed the production facility for the wholesale operations before they were relocated to New Jersey. On the ground floor was an unimpressive retail store that mirrored the 80th Street location in dank disrepair and lack of amenities. On the roof were two advertising billboards, which faced the West Side Highway and generated close to $30,000 a month in rent for Helmer Toro. While buildings in the area were being forced to remove their billboards by New York City, the Toro billboards were "grandfathered in", securing their presence and increasing their value.

Once the production facility was relocated, Helmer proceeded to sublet the rest of the building to two commissaries for pushcart vendors. This became the central place on the west side of Manhattan that pushcart vendors went to restock and to store their equipment. The major problem with this tenancy was two-fold. The first was that the rent Helmer was charging, which was often unpaid, was below market value. The second was that it created a filthy, unsanitary, rat, roach, and fly infested environment in the building. The sheer volume of pushcarts made it completely unmanageable.

The building's unique character, size, and layout made it a valuable piece of New York City real estate. The building was close to being owned free and clear by one of the Toro Limited Partnerships when Helmer stripped all of the equity in order to finance the Jersey acquisition and freezer excavation.

By the time they arrived at the store, the New York State Finance Enforcement agents had already cleared the premises of all the workers and customers. They were in the process of placing large orange delinquency stickers in the window. These agents were awaiting the arrival of a locksmith to change the locks when Marcus and Toro got the scene. Helmer greeted the agents cordially, and turned over the funds to them in exchange for their calling off the seizure. It was such a simple transaction. Helmer clearly had the funds. So why let it get to this stage? Marcus couldn't begin to conjecture. Maybe he just lived for the thrill of it all.

Helmer, in typical fashion, looked across the store at the numerous members of the New York State Finance Department's task force and said, generally, to the group, "Go ahead. Have a bagel. It's on me."

Chapter 11

January 2011-Helmer and Brian sat next to each other on one side of a large, mahogany conference room table. Marcus sat in a swivel chair against the wall, not far from where his employer and company counsel were sitting. He was relegated to carrying the mass of file boxes that were necessary for the matter at hand. George Surgent, attorney for Amy Toro, sat a few seats away from Helmer, but on the same side of the table. Dr. Amy Dukoff-Toro was not present. She remained in New York.

The H&H legal department had flown to Miami, Florida to take the deposition of Robert Benjamin, the plaintiff in a series of equipment leasing lawsuits that were brought in Hudson County, New Jersey against Helmer's entities, Helmer Toro, personally, and Amy Dukoff-Toro as Limited Partner. It was these legal matters that had Amy screaming the day Marcus had met her in her apartment, and, quite frankly, every single day that Marcus reported to work there.

Robert Benjamin was a snow-bird. He spent his summers in New York and winters in Florida. He was in his 80's and was now too ill to fly to New Jersey for the deposition in the dead of winter. In consideration of his condition, the Court allowed the deposition to occur closer to Benjamin's Florida home.

Bob Benjamin was a retired equipment financier. He had a 30-year business relationship and friendship with Helmer Toro, and had provided substantial financing to Helmer's businesses over the years. Helmer would attend bagel equipment auctions with a figurative blank check from Bob and bid on everything in sight. Much of what he purchased he did not even have any use for, and consequently was part of what constituted much of the junk Marcus had witnesses at 35 UPS Drive. Marcus recognized that when it came to other people's money, Helmer was not particularly prudent about what he spent it on. As Marcus had heard him say so often, "It's okay, it's Bob's money."

Bob's financing was not limited only to bagel equipment. The two cars that Helmer rode around the city in were both financed by Bob. Most significantly, when Helmer got arrested for tax fraud in 2009 and the New York State Finance Department had padlocked Helmer's West 46th Street location, it was Bob who wired Helmer the $100,000 needed to get the store re-opened. Bob did it with no questions asked and without even getting a promissory note signed. He trusted Helmer Toro.

Bob Benjamin was owed almost $1.5 million dollars at the time that Helmer stopped paying, and he had no intention of simply walking away from it. Bob filed lawsuits in Hudson County, New Jersey to collect his money from all of the related H&H entities, as well as Helmer Toro individually. The obvious problem with suing Helmer Toro was that he owned nothing in his name, and whatever he did own had tax liens affixed to it, which took legal priority. This didn't deter Bob from proceeding.

Bob was the first creditor of the H&H family of businesses that conceived of going after Amy to recover his debt. This was what distinguished Bob's case from all the ones where creditors saw no point in proceeding and getting a worthless paper judgment. Bob's cleverly crafted attack on Amy is what made his litigation so contentious. It was also precedent setting. If Bob was able to pierce Amy's blanket of protection, all of the other creditors would immediately follow suit under the same premise.

Under most analysis of the law, Limited Partners are insulated from the liabilities of the partnership. Limited Partners stand in the shoes of a silent investor and they give up decision-making authority to the General Partner. The Limited Partner does stand to become personally liable, however, when they violate their role as a silent partner. When these Limited Partners become involved in the running of the business and the decision-making process, they are equally as culpable as the General Partner. This was the basis upon which Bob Benjamin used to go after Amy

Toro personally. He believed that Amy Toro was actively engaged in the decision making process with her husband at H&H. If Bob was correct in his claim, he would have a greater chance of collecting any judgment rendered in his favor, as she was a much more financially viable defendant than her well-insulated husband.

To say that Amy Toro did not deal well with being sued personally would be a gross understatement of the facts. Amy hired several attorneys, firing those that did not agree with her perspective on the case and those that refused to hear her repeated attestations about her legal understanding of the case, despite the fact that it might have contradicted the law. She also took offensive measures against Bob, filing money laundering, criminal usury, and tax evasion complaints against Bob in the hopes of scaring him off. At one point, the U.S. Government even froze Bob's assets, which they later released, as part of their investigation into his relationship with Helmer.

During the hours that Marcus was with Helmer and Amy there was not one moment that she did not talk about the case. She talked about why she was wronged and how she was going to seek retribution against all those involved, including Helmer and H&H's former Attorney, Jorge Delgado. For Marcus, the most difficult aspect of dealing with Amy was that when he disagreed with her she always said the same thing:

"You don't understand what I am saying."

Marcus always understood, but often he did not agree. It seemed making this distinction was a futile exercise.

The tactics used to defend against Bob's lawsuits ran the gamut, from simple legal defenses, to claims of civil and criminal usury and beyond. The cases against Helmer were filed in New Jersey, which was where the equipment was now located, so Helmer filed a series of independent cases in New York State, as the Plaintiff, under a different set of corporate entities than those that were being sued in New Jersey. He brought many of the same causes of action he had crafted as defenses in the Jersey case in order to force the sickly Bob Benjamin to fight on two geographic fronts.

Helmer employed Machiavellian measures to frustrate the efforts of Benjamin and Friedrich. Helmer viewed the removal of Judge Suarez in the Hudson County case as paramount to having any success there. Judge Suarez was a no-nonsense Judge that had expressed contempt for Helmer's delays, antics, and repeated failures to adhere to Court imposed deadlines. In order to address the issue, Helmer coordinated the engagement of new Counsel for Amy. He researched and deliberately hired a partner from the same law firm as Judge Suarez to act as Amy's new co-Counsel. Helmer's team then filed a conflict motion, asking the Judge to recuse herself, arguing that as Amy and Helmer had adverse claims he could never get a fair trial with the Judge and Amy's partner being from the same law firm. Although Judge Suarez could have denied the motion, she voluntarily recused herself from hearing the case in order to avoid the appearance of impropriety. A new Judge was appointed and Helmer's immediate problem was solved. Marcus now saw that Helmer would go to any extreme to achieve a goal he thought worthy. Marcus found himself to be both impressed and frightened by Helmer's "take no prisoners" approach.

Marcus' impression of Robert Benjamin was that he was a distinguished, kindly gentleman, who had a no-nonsense approach to his business. While Marcus had the impression that Robert must have worked hard in his life, he gave the appearance that he was affluent. Not generational money, but moneyed nonetheless, Marcus supposed.

As for Bob's attorney, Jay Friedrich, he was among the most unappealing, vulgar, and brash people Marcus had ever laid eyes on. He was loud and unnecessarily rude to the people surrounding Helmer, as if he held them accountable for Helmer's behavior. This was especially evident in his abusive treatment of Helmer's young Counsel, Brian Confino. Brian was a good and decent man but he was relatively inexperienced and had a passive demeanor. Jay proceeded to bully and insult him at every opportunity.

In fairness to Jay Friedrich, Marcus thought to himself, it seemed that Helmer managed to have the ability to bring out the worst in people. Perhaps Friedrich was angry that Helmer tried to have him removed as Counsel, claiming he had previously been Helmer's lawyer too. Perhaps he was angry that Helmer filed ethics complaints against him with the Bar Association and was trying to have his license revoked. Perhaps he was just frustrated from Helmer and Amy's escalation of simple contract lawsuits into so much more. Regardless, his behavior was not reflective of a professional attorney advocating for his client, but that of an aggrieved party with a visible ax to grind.

The parties spent a good part of the day locked in this conference room, questioning Bob Benjamin about his business history and relationship to the Toros and H&H. Brian nervously questioned Bob while Jay Friedrich screamed and threw papers about, threatening to end the deposition and seek sanctions after almost every question. The Court Reporter looked on in amusement. Marcus was certain that this was more entertaining than the normal, boring depositions he was used to.

Brian Confino forged ahead, red in the face from embarrassment and discomfort. Amy's attorney also questioned Bob on the record, about the basis for his allegations that Amy was somehow involved in the decision-making process at H&H. Bob's burden of proof was extremely high, and Surgent, who was a seasoned legal practitioner, attempted to illicit what, if any, information Bob could assert to back his claims. Unlike when Brian Confino was doing the questioning, when Surgent proceeded Jay Friedrich exercised a bit more self-control.

As the afternoon wore on, Bob decided he had had enough. Marcus wasn't sure if the adjournment was the result of physical or emotional fatigue, but the result was the same nonetheless. The deposition was over. Bob said his goodbyes and left with Friedrich hot on his tail.

As an exhausted, battered Brian Confino, with Marcus' assistance, gathered up his files, he appeared to have been physically battered rather than simply verbally. He seemed to be suffering from a combination of fatigue and PTSD. Helmer, meanwhile, got up and looked over at his team with a huge, sheepish grin on his face.

"Who's up for some Miami nightlife?"

Chapter 12

"H&H backer bankrupt and $5 Million in debt."- **NY Post, February 19, 2011**

By the time four months of Marcus' new employment with the Toro Empire had passed, he had become an expert in all things H&H. He understood the structure, the history, and even the personalities of the major players. He also began to understand the complex and unusual mind of its Chief Operating Officer; the man called "El Jefe."

As a student of H&H, Marcus understood that February 18, 2011 was the most significant date in the history of the company to that point. That was the date that Garden Operation Realty, the entity that managed the property at 35 UPS Drive, filed for bankruptcy protection under Chapter 11 of the Federal Bankruptcy Code. Helmer could no longer fight the onslaught of litigation over the property, including the Benjamin lawsuits. Additionally, the foreclosure and subsequent evictions were no longer manageable with Helmer's persuasive stalling tactics and promises to pay. All the legal filibustering to delay the proceedings had also run its course. But for this legal maneuver, the property would have been lost to creditors within days. The automatic stay in Federal Bankruptcy put a hold on all legal proceedings involving the entity, including all state eviction and foreclosure proceedings. Helmer always felt that buying time would allow for a great opportunity to be revealed. Marcus knew that no one was better at buying time than Helmer Toro.

As Marcus worked together with Helmer's counsel of choice, the esteemed Lexington Avenue law firm of Randy Kornfeld & Associates, to put the paperwork together for the Chapter 11 filing, a few things became abundantly clear to him.

The first revelation was that, whether by design or omission, the business records for H&H Bagels' companies were a complete and total disaster. Helmer moved money, employees, and assets from one company to another like they were checkers on a board. It was extremely difficult to reconstruct the records required by the Bankruptcy Court, in its standard oversight, to determine the viability of the business. Many of the employees had recently been moved on paper to New Jersey Companies in order to thwart the Manhattan DA's investigation of payroll issues and employee leasing agreements in New York.

Additionally, employees were rarely paid with a normal paycheck. They often received a payment voucher, which they would submit to one of the retail locations or the corporate office for cash payments. Often there was no notation of the number of hours worked, the rate of pay, or their withholding information. They also often didn't receive the full amount they were due on their scheduled payday. They would receive a partial sum and replacement voucher, with the remaining balance noted, for cashing at a later date. One of the most troubling aspects of the system was that none of the vouchers actually indicated which company they worked for, leaving all the employees to say they worked for H&H.

Marcus also learned from the filing how profoundly the creditors of H&H and Helmer Toro distrusted and disliked him, particularly at the Internal Revenue Service, a major creditor of the H&H Empire.

Marcus attended a preliminary conference of the bankruptcy creditors with Randy Kornfeld. The IRS and their lawyers, the Justice Department, also attended this conference. During the course of the meeting, the IRS representative passionately outlined the frustration the U.S. Government had experienced in the many years of chasing Helmer Toro. She went on to say that on behalf of the taxpayers she hadn't eaten a bagel in ten years, because the sight of one reminded her of H&H and it made her physically sick. Marcus was floored by her candor and by the levels of animus that people felt towards his notorious employer. Marcus was also starting to learn that the dislike for Helmer came from many different and diverse areas. He found the agent's anger a stark contrast to Helmer's dismissive comments on his own tax liability.

"When you owe the government a million dollars, it's your problem. When you owe the government $20 million dollars it's their problem," he would mockingly pontificate.

The final thing that was revealed to Marcus through the bankruptcy filing was the power of, belief in, and devotion to the H&H brand from a marketing standpoint. Every major news outlet picked up on the filing, and within 24-hours all of the headlines read about how the famed bagel maker had filed for bankruptcy protection. Every news outlet was speculating whether this would mean the end of this beloved, household brand.

As a result of all of the publicity, venture capitalists, angel investors, food conglomerates, bagel chains, mortgage lenders, and other interested parties all raced to try to make a deal to save the brand. For Helmer Toro, the trouble in New Jersey opened an entire window of opportunity for the future.

Chapter 13

Helmer was a man who was never without a plan. Now was no different. His simple plan to save H&H from Bankruptcy was to find a willing investor to license the brand to for $50 million dollars. For that sum, the licensee would get the use of the brand via a long-term license, leases to the two parcels of real estate H&H owned, the 80th street lease, the use of the intellectual property, including the logo, slogan, and phone number, 1-800-NY BAGEL, and use of the secret formula. The successful bidder would need to pay Helmer 14% royalties based on gross sales for the duration of the license, and provide Helmer with a lifetime consulting agreement. The consulting contract would afford a $125,000 base salary plus provide two vehicles, expenses, a cell phone, and medical benefits for the family. Helmer saw it all as very reasonable.

Marcus saw some difficulties with the proposal, however. His initial thought was that no one would actually pay $50 million for the right to use the brand. It just wasn't worth it. Even if the buildings were included, they were only valued at $20 million, maximum. However, the title to the buildings was not included for this sum, just a leasehold interest in them with the rent being paid to Toro.

As for the royalties, it was common knowledge that most food related businesses survive on 20% profit or less. For the licensee to pay 14% to Helmer in royalties would have been unprecedented, and also would have clearly had Helmer making more money than the company that bought him out.

Finally, while there may have been some value to having Helmer stay on board during a transition, it was unlikely that anyone would want to be married to him for life, especially with the sizable package he proposed.

Helmer tried to tip the scales in his favor by looking to partner with a venture capitalist rather than a food industry candidate. He was highly suspicious of food people, and Marcus suspected that he knew food people would not need him long term. A financier would have the funds to proceed, but would need to rely on Helmer for the knowledge of the business. In Helmer's mind, to a financier he was indispensable.

On this morning, Marcus was walking behind Helmer along Columbus Circle as Helmer kept to the shadows of the city skyscrapers. Helmer told Marcus that his exposure to the chemical Agent Orange in Vietnam destroyed his pigmentation, making him susceptible to severe sun damage – hence the need to walk in the shadows whenever possible. Marcus admired Helmer's service in Vietnam, but he couldn't help but thinking that Helmer must have seen some angle in it or he would have found a way to get out of it.

Helmer broke his dress protocol this morning and put on a navy blue blazer with gold buttons over his print, button shirt. He was certain that there was a dress code at the Mandarin Oriental Hotel, where they were having breakfast with an interested investor. They didn't want to get turned away over their appearance. In preparation for the meeting,

Helmer called Marcus no less than 5 times to remind him not to wear jeans to the meeting. Marcus took it in stride, despite the fact that he never wore jeans to work.

Gryfe's of Canada was a 90-year old, reputable business establishment that was comprised of wholesale and retail bagel operations. It was a successful operation and, despite being twice as old as Helmer's establishment, was known as "Canada's H&H." This in and of itself showed the power of the H&H brand internationally.

Daniel Gryfe, the grandson of the founder, spent time in the States every year because his wife was originally from New York. He had scheduled a meeting with Helmer to discuss a possible North American merger. Helmer listened attentively over breakfast, as Gryfe gave his background, explained about his operation, and discussed the potential of a merger. When Gryfe had finished, he looked to Helmer for his thoughts.

"Well, sounds nice. Sounds nice." At this point Helmer's voice dropped and he mumbled slightly as he said, "In order to proceed with the discussions I would need a $50,000 non-refundable deposit."

"Excuse me? I could not hear you."

Helmer repeated the request again, to which Gryfe repeated his request for clarity. It was at this time that Marcus, as he had become accustomed to doing, became the translator.

"Helmer says in order to proceed with discussions he would require a $50,000, non-refundable deposit."

"Is that a serious request?"

"Yes."

"Helmer, do I look stupid to you? Do I not appear serious? You realize this breakfast just cost me $900?"

"Well, those are my terms."

"Helmer. I am a good guy to do business with. This is a great opportunity for both of us, but I am not the one in bankruptcy. I am leaving here in two days. If I don't hear from you by then I will assume we have nothing further to talk about. Regardless, there will be no non-refundable deposit."

"How about $10,000?"

"Helmer, how about $0!"

With that the meeting was over. Gryfe departed from their company and no further negotiations took place.

Marcus looked at Helmer.

"They might be worth talking to, Helmer. They have a thriving business and obviously they are successful. He seems like a serious guy."

"Kid, they just wanna steal my secret formula."

Chapter 14

In order to be able to sustain a viable plan in Bankruptcy, the debtor needs to demonstrate that they are a running their business in a sustainable manner and that they can afford any reorganization plan the Court approves. H&H could do neither.

Helmer, despite the numerous requests of the Trustee, Greg Zipes, and his own attorney, Randy Kornfeld, was completely unable to provide any substantial financial records relating to conduct of the business of the debtor. Of all of the documents requested, only a handful of checklist items were partially submitted. Helmer kept stalling. He used the excuse that the accounting department was on vacation. Then he fired one of the accounting employees and put forth that this employee was the only one with access to the records. The excuses were piling up, and the deadlines set by the Court were summarily being ignored.

In addition, in order for the plan to be approved, the debtor would need to demonstrate that it had an ability to make the reorganization payments required under the plan. There were no real tenants at the Jersey property, and Helmer's entity was financially strapped. He could support no claims of an ability to make any payments under the plan. No documentation could support it.

The end result of all of these issues was that while the bankruptcy proceeding did stall the state legal proceedings against H&H, it did not resolve anything. Judge Sean H. Lane lifted any automatic stay against the creditors and allowed the liquidation of the New Jersey property to proceed. The 75,000 square foot behemoth that housed the freezer of tomorrow was soon no longer part of the H&H family and never would be again.

Helmer quickly gave orders, despite Court directives to the contrary, to strip the Jersey facility of all of the equipment and materials the workers could before the sheriffs came to lock the place up. They managed to move a substantial amount of the functioning equipment back to West 46th Street, the prior site of years of manufacturing. To their credit, within days the workers moved and re-assembled most of the Jersey equipment and were back to producing a substantial amount of the wholesale bagel orders from the 46th Street bakery. The moved equipment was all the subject of Bob Benjamin's case in Hudson County, making the assignment and transfer to New York State from New Jersey another complication in the Jersey Court case.

Meanwhile, the flagship store on 80th Street was in serious trouble. Helmer had fallen behind in making rent payments, to the tune of over $400,000. Friedland Properties, the landlord, commenced eviction proceedings after a series of negotiated settlements between Helmer and Friedland's agents, which, of course, Helmer broke.

As judgment day approached for the most famous bagel store in the world, Helmer devised a new scenario that would transform his financial plight into a battle of good versus evil.

Chapter 15

March 2011- After exhausting all of his remedies in Landlord and Tenant Court to save the flagship store from eviction, Helmer decided it was time to file another bankruptcy proceeding. From his experience with the New Jersey property Helmer was smart enough to recognize that filing was only a stop-gap measure. There would be no way to propose a viable financial plan for this property either, and he faced similar problems over the lack of adequate financial records to support the legitimacy of the business.

Helmer understood that a bankruptcy attorney as sophisticated as Randy Kornfeld would be reluctant to appear before a Federal Judge in another "bad" H&H case. Additionally, Kornfeld's fees were sizable. Randy was not enamored enough by Helmer's quasi-celebrity status to take less, and the Bankruptcy Court rules did not allow the fees to be made after the filing. Kornfeld insisted on being paid his standard fee before the case was filed. Helmer's solution was to identify an attorney who was beguiled by the fame of H&H, but who had little experience in the sophisticated world of Chapter 11 filings and re-organization plans. That attorney, Mel Gonzalez, raced to the Federal Courthouse to file another "just in the nick of time" bankruptcy proceeding, this time on behalf of the First Toro – the 80th Street operating entity.

The second filing had two major implications. The first was to infuriate the creditors, many of whom were the same ones for the Jersey case. The second was to infuriate the Court. The Federal Courts very strictly address frivolous filings. They abhor the use of the court system as a means of personal obfuscation. This second "shell" filing, with a legal practitioner not readily known to the Court or Trustee, made apparent what was going on.

Meanwhile, the additional press coverage of the second filing actually increased the interest of buyers and investors. These financial strategists presumed they would now have a greater probability of being able to bring Helmer to the bargaining table than they did after the Jersey filing. Surely, they thought, he would rather make a deal than lose the foundation of his international business enterprise.

80th Street, after all, had become a New York City landmark. Not only was it known all over the world, the subject of cinematic and television coverage, and a regular spot on every New York City sightseeing tour, but it had also been single handedly responsible for the coronation of the Upper West Side as the bagel capital of the world. As far as Marcus was concerned, without 80th Street, there was no H&H.

Helmer and Marcus attended one investor meeting after another, all with similar outcomes. People formulated creative and bold plans for mergers, co-branding, franchising, and more, only to walk away from the meetings in utter disbelief over Helmer's intransigence and increasingly outrageous terms.

One tenacious, mid-western venture capitalist was Marc Halpern. Halpern was intimately aware of H&H's brand appeal and production capacity from his years of working in the mid-west distribution chain of the organization. He also was a resourceful entrepreneur that managed to put several serious investment groups together to propose saving H&H. Each meeting was more frustrating than the next, but Halpern pressed on, believing he could save H&H. His fortitude was a close match to Helmer's. However, while Marc was schooled in many economic fundamentals, this was his first exposure to an economic theory that Marcus later referred to as "Helmer-nomics".

"Helmer, I am confused. You just lost 75,000 square feet. Your ability to produce is diminished substantially. 80th Street's eviction is only a matter of time and you just raised the stakes for a deal? What gives?"

"Marc, it's the law of supply and demand. We are more valuable now than ever."

"Helmer, what are you going to do once the retail stores end up closing?"

"Marc, let me ask you a question," Helmer said. Once again, his voice was reduced to a quiet mumble.

"How many retail stores does Coca-Cola have?"

"Sorry, Helmer. I am not following."

"How many retail stores does Coca-Cola have?" he repeated.

"I really can't understand what you are saying."

With that Marcus jumped in. By now, he understood Helmer's unique way of thinking.

"He is asking how many retail stores Coca-Cola has. The answer is obviously none. Yet, they are sold all over the world. He is suggesting the retail store is not essential to the success of the brand."

"Helmer, is that a serious question? Is that a serious analogy? Coca-Cola has one of the strongest brands and strongest distribution chains in the world. How is it comparable?"

"Marc, we're the Google of bagels."

"I am sorry?"

"We're the Google of bagels."

Before Marc Halpern could ask again Marcus interrupted, "Helmer is suggesting H&H is the Google of bagels."

This ended the meeting, but not Halpern's interest or attempts to bring viable deals to Toro in the hopes that he would become more intellectually pliable at some point. Marcus felt that Helmer never had the proper respect for Halpern to treat his proposals with any serious consideration. He just enjoyed going through the exercise of having Halpern pitch another variation of a deal.

As Helmer was speaking to interested parties, he was simultaneously conducting research on every company that had sold or licensed its brand in modern history, and had legally taken it back after the sale by voiding the contract or filing litigation. Although he was not a formally educated person, Helmer was an extremely clever and resourceful guy. Helmer thought by studying these cases he would be able to have the license documents drafted in such a way that would make it easier for him to recapture the brand from the buyer at a later date. Marcus came to understand that Helmer never entered into any contract that he didn't intend to breach. It was standard operating procedure for him.

Chapter 16

As the summer months approached, the Bankruptcy Court lifted the automatic stay in the 80th Street case in order to allow an eviction to proceed. With no deal even close to being formulated, Helmer began to show subtle signs of desperation. In addition to these issues, the IRS was becoming more aggressive, and with the New Jersey stay lifted, Benjamin and Friedrich were engaged in a full court press against Helmer and Amy in Hudson County. With the promise of a $1.5 million dollar personal judgment against Amy in Hudson County, she became even more relentless in her harassment of Helmer, Marcus, and Brian Confino. She was demanding that she be exculpated from liability. Amy's morning and evening tirades were interspersed with a flurry of repetitive phone calls throughout the day on the same subject. These calls all involved Amy outlining in detail, and repeating, all the reasons why she should have no liability in the case, and threatening the consequences if she did.

One May morning, after the cars were all secure and breakfast was consumed, Helmer handed Marcus a white, standard sized envelope and a paper with a handwritten address on it.

"I need you to go to this address and stick this letter in the doorman's hand with a $20 bill."

"What is it?"

"It's a letter for Seinfeld."

"Are you serious? Helmer? Seinfeld? Jerry Seinfeld? Saying what?"

"Go ahead, read it."

Marcus opened the unsealed envelope and unfolded the handwritten letter. The letter opened with a very brief reference to H&H's recent troubles and then went on to remind Jerry Seinfeld that he made a significant amount of money over the years using the H&H brand in his episode, "The Strike." As a result, Helmer felt it was only fair that Jerry extend a low interest loan to H&H to save it from its current legal troubles. It went on to say what great publicity it would be for Seinfeld and H&H.

Marcus completed reading the letter. He folded it and reinserted it into the envelope. He looked Helmer dead in the eyes and asked, "Are you serious with this?"

"Yeah, yeah, yeah. Go ahead. He is gonna love it."

As with so many of the tasks Marcus was charged within his employment with H&H, he proceeded, despite his embarrassment, out of a sense of duty to his employer. Marcus reluctantly delivered the letter to Jerry Seinfeld's doorman at a luxury building in Manhattan. He had no way of knowing for sure where Helmer got Seinfeld's address from and if it was a reliable source. The Doorman took the letter from Marcus, but refused the money. Marcus was never sure if it really was Seinfeld's doorman, or if the letter ever got to Seinfeld, but they never heard a thing about it again.

Chapter 17

June 2011- Since being notified that the Federal Judge was lifting the automatic stay in the 80th Street case and that the eviction would be proceeding, Helmer and Marcus racked their brains to construct a plan to save the store. There were no more legal maneuvers to utilize in the State or Federal Courts, and there were no buyers ready to proceed.

Marcus urged Helmer to focus all of his attention on saving the retail store. He believed that the 80th Street store was the cornerstone and building block of the entire organization. If Helmer saved 80th, even if it meant sacrificing the wholesale operation, it would be a place to rebuild. 80th Street had become part of the fabric of the neighborhood and New York City, itself.

"The biggest shame of all of this is that the whole Upper West Side really is losing its essential character. It's starting to look like everywhere else in the city. After H&H closes, the Friedlands will just put up a drug store or a cell phone store there. Too bad we don't have some landmark protections."

"That's it," Helmer responded.

"No Helmer. Landmark protection runs with the building, not a store. Too bad, though."

Helmer became quiet, obviously deep in thought.

"I have a plan," Helmer muttered.

"Okay, shoot."

"What if we started a 'Save H&H' campaign? What if we put out there the notion that this wasn't about money at all, but that we were being forced out so the Friedlands could rent the property to a big corporate tenant like Walgreens or Wal-Mart? People here would hate it. They want the neighborhood to stay small, with its own unique character. They would rally to keep us open."

Marcus thought about it for a moment and realized it was actually a really good idea. It might not work, but it would be great publicity, and it was the publicity that kept drawing in all the potential investors. Despite all of its issues, H&H was still a darling with the news media. The Press loved H&H stories, even if those stories weren't so newsworthy. This one actually had some sex appeal.

Since Helmer's indictment, he had been reluctant to provide any interviews or allow any media access, despite the delicate and reverential manner with which most members of the Press still approached H&H stories. "No comment," was his standard reply to every request for information, big or small. There was always some element of reverence in them. However, in this case he knew it would be a story that would have a favorable angle.

"I like it, Helmer."

Helmer snickered to himself, enjoying Marcus' approval.

Marcus proceeded to prepare and circulate a few Press Releases framing the story, and made a few calls to media outlets like **DNAinfo** and **The West Side Rag**. These local news outlets were always focused on preserving the essential character of New York City's neighborhoods. They were very intrigued by the David and Goliath angle. Friedland Properties became objectified as the enemy of the average New Yorker in virtually every story.

On June 27, 2011, media, concerned citizens, and other onlookers gathered in Riverside Park on what was a beautiful, sunny day. The afternoon was filled with inspiring speeches and memories shared by young professionals that literally teethed on H&H bagels in the 1970's and 1980's. People rallied and held up signs that said "SAVE H&H." Marcus was astounded by the power that this brand had to inspire people. He also couldn't help but wonder how many of them would be at the rally if they had any idea what Helmer Toro was really like.

Even Marc Halpern attended the rally, as did Evan Giniger, a New York City design architect who had been part of the investment group trying to license the H&H brand. Giniger, a believer that H&H was part of modern New York City heritage, later went on to buy the historic Lower East Side Kossar's Bialy's to preserve it from extinction.

The event was a terrific and notable photo opportunity and news story. Coverage was widespread. It was all over the television, internet, and appeared in all major newspapers. However, it raised no money and it did nothing to save the historic bagel seller.

Two days later, the City Marshal showed up with a Warrant of Eviction and Judgment of Possession and proceeded to seize and lock up the beloved bagel store that Helmer Toro had wrestled from his brother, Phillip, so many years ago. While Helmer had been on the brink of disaster many other times over the years, this was the first time he couldn't find a way to save this cornerstone of his empire.

At the time the Marshal came to 80th Street to commence the eviction, the store was filled with lines of people that actually extended onto Broadway. These loyal patrons had made a pilgrimage to the store to stock up, and fill their freezers, with H&H bagels before they became a scarcity. People actually cried at the news of the store closing. People made special trips to see the shuttered icon one last time. Adults and children alike took to the internet and posted videos and songs on **YouTube**, paying homage to a store that they took for granted would always be a part of their community. While Marcus and Helmer publically vilified the Friedlands, they knew in their hearts that it was Helmer who was solely responsible for eradicating this community gathering place from the people of the Upper West Side.

The shuttering of H&H's retail store was permanent. 2239 W. Broadway would soon be excavated in preparation for the arrival of new Verizon Mobile store where the bagel maker used to sit, across from the historic and beloved Zabar's, just as Marcus had predicted.

Just eight months after Marcus had met Helmer and come aboard as a key employee of this legendary institution of New York City, the New Jersey wholesale factory was gone, the flagship store in New York City was gone, and the corporate offices were gone. Simultaneously, the Internal Revenue Service was seeking 20 million dollars in back taxes. Judgment creditors were closing in as Helmer Toro made one last play to save his remaining building, retail store, and tarnished yet valued brand.

Chapter 18

It was one month from the day that the 80th Street Store was shuttered that Helmer, reunited with attorney Randy Kornfield, appeared before Judge Sean Lane in the Federal Bankruptcy Court of the Southern District on a creditor's motion to convert a new Chapter 11 filing from a re-organization to a liquidation. The Petitioner this time was the entity known as the Third Toro. This was the holding company that owned the real property on West 46th Street.

Unlike the other Chapter 11 filings, there were actually assets associated with this corporation. Despite heavy leveraging of the equity in the building, its location and unique characteristics made it valuable enough that a court ordered appraisal revealed there would be assets after a sale for the creditors to fight over.

Normally, Helmer waited until the last opportunity to file any legal papers. He was notorious for getting to the courthouse just before it closed on the day papers were due to be submitted. This was a strategy largely designed to give his numerous adversaries as little time as possible to review and defend his often outlandish claims. Helmer filed this bankruptcy a little earlier than he would have otherwise for one simple reason. In the New York City's Commercial Landlord and Tenant Court, a Receiver had been judicially appointed to collect the sizable rents from the tenants, especially the Wagner Billboards positioned along the West Side Highway. Helmer had managed to collect those rents himself, and somehow neglected to turn over the funds to the appointed Receiver. A furious New York City Judge set a court date for Helmer to appear and deliver the rents. She was threatening to hold Helmer in contempt of Court and throw him in The Tombs Prison until he came up with the funds. This, rather than the pending foreclosure, was the real impetus to file for bankruptcy protection when he did. Helmer calculated correctly that the authority of the Federal Judge would supersede the City, and the issue of the misappropriated rents would be lost in the other chaos associated with another Toro bankruptcy filing. Helmer never was called to account for these rents again.

In the months prior to the liquidation of West 46th Street, Helmer had met with numerous potential partners, including the young, charming real estate mogul, Michael Shah, of DelShah Capital. Michael promulgated a complex plan to purchase the building, keep H&H open, and offer some financial relief to the creditors. The Bankruptcy Court and Trustee rejected the DelShah plan, however, as not offering enough assets to other creditors after the sale.

Simultaneously, Helmer and Marcus continued to entertain numerous offers to keep the brand alive. The most promising of these offers came from an international coffee chain centered on the West Coast that was looking to launch, starting in New York City, a chain of co-branded H&H coffee shops. The CEO, with an impressive résumé as a real estate developer and owner of 275 Nursing Homes, flew in from

California to try to talk sensibly to Helmer about a realistic and viable deal. With only 2-3% royalties being offered, little upfront money, and only 3 years as a consultant commitment, Helmer walked away from the deal, which did not surprise Marcus.

What this recent deal rejection did do for Marcus was to confirm for him that if Judge Lane approved the conversion of the Third Toro bankruptcy from reorganization to liquidation, it would just be a matter of time before H&H completely ceased to exist.

Marcus couldn't help thinking of something Marc Halpern had said to him about Helmer's intransigence: "H&H will be like Prodigy. Remember, Prodigy, the Search Engine software? They were big once. Just a memory now."

Halpern was right. Chances were that the biggest bagel brand in the world was on life support and fading fast.

Chapter 19

As time passed there were many times that Marcus felt that he had gained a better understanding of the complex and unusual mind of Helmer Toro. Many times in meetings, he knew the direction that Helmer would take before he ever uttered a word. Other times, Marcus was at a complete loss. There were times that he felt there must have been a thoughtful and calculated agenda that underlined the way that Helmer behaved. Other times, he felt that Helmer proceeded in a random and chaotic matter that was outside of the scope of Marcus' comprehension. Marcus often, in his own insecurity, felt it was his own shortcomings that did not allow him to see the picture with the certainty and surety with which Helmer proceeded. There were some occasions, however, that Marcus did feel certain that there was no logic to the madness he was surrounded with.

As Marcus sat across from Helmer in their newly retrofitted, West Side office, the receiving department began to unload large flat boxes from a third party's delivery vehicle. Helmer was visibly excited by the arrival. He knew instantly what the packages contained. As he unfolded his pocketknife and began to cut open one of the large boxes, Marcus grew very curious.

"What did you get, Helmer?"

"This is so great. I have been waiting for this. Wait till you see this. It is so cool!"

With that, Helmer removed the cardboard and inner packing materials, revealing a large, Lucite panel decorated with photographs of H&H bagels. It contained some strategically located cutouts. The decorated panel was about 6 feet long and 3.5 feet wide.

"What is that?" Marcus inquired.

"You really don't know?"

"Helmer, I have no idea."

"This is the front panel of the new H&H Bagel vending machines. I ordered 100 of them to start."

"100 what? Vending machines?"

"No, just the panels."

"Helmer, where are the machines they go with?"

"Oh, they don't exist yet. These are just prototypes of the fronts. I am going to use them to get the machines made."

"If there are no machines yet, how did you figure the size and dimensions?"

"I just took the dimensions off of the soda vending machine in my building. It's got to be a standard size, I think."

Marcus was completely unsure of how to respond. The company was in a major economic crisis, being fought on numerous fronts, and its Chief Executive was spending money on decorative panels for bagel vending machines that did not exist and were not on the horizon.

"Is it just me?" Marcus considered.

Chapter 20

August 2011- In the days after Judge Lane's conversion of the Third Toro case, things continued to spiral downward in the H&H world, not just for the company, but for the employees and their families. Many of the workers had been with Helmer for years, and they trusted him. They believed he would never let them down. They were wrong.

Marcus knew the end was in sight but he held out hope that Helmer would come to his senses and that they could make a deal with one of the many, eager investors that were still vying for the opportunity to resuscitate the brand. Marcus and the other workers continued to work, even though they had not been paid, literally, in weeks.

While H&H was still producing and selling bagels, there were times that they were selling them at a financial loss. The four major flour suppliers in the country all revoked Helmer Toro's credit terms. Instead of being able to have security in a negotiated price for flour based upon volume, Helmer was required to call every morning to order small amounts of flour at the day's market price. He was then required to wire transfer "good funds" to the mill. Once the funds cleared, he was allowed to pick up the daily flour order at the mill. As with any commodity, the market price can fluctuate significantly from day to day. Therefore, there were some days that the cost of producing bagels far exceeded the sale price. Helmer's response was to raise bagel prices 40% across the board, making his wholesale bagel price equivalent to buying retail. This major price increase caused even the most loyal customers to seek other suppliers to sustain their own businesses. There was no longer any money in wholesalers reselling H&H bagels, despite any demand by end users. Another H&H revenue stream had now dried up. Another domino had fallen. The end of the road was quickly approaching.

The financial strain on the H&H employees' families was starting to take a human toll that no longer made Helmer's quirky, eccentric approach to life amusing. Marcus was at the center of fielding the pained calls of workers, and it was taking its toll on him emotionally.

Carlos Torres, a loyal and long-time employee in the accounting department, called Marcus in tears.

"Marcus, do you know anything about our health insurance being cancelled?"

"No, why?"

"Marcus, I have cancer and I had an operation scheduled. I had to cancel it because the surgeon is saying I have no health insurance. There has to be some mistake, right?"

"Must be an error. Let me look into it. I will call you back."

Sadly, it was no error. Helmer had deducted the medical insurance premiums from the workers' pay, and, much like the withholding taxes, he never remitted them to the health insurance company. Marcus was heart-broken. He had to call Carlos back to inform him that he would be unable to schedule his cancer operation. This was the low point for Marcus. Now, it wasn't simply about money and bagels. Now, the impact of Helmer's antics was the decimation of lives and health.

The financial strain on the workers was continuing to take its toll. Despite the frustration of these workers, most that were living paycheck to paycheck, they still trusted Helmer's word that it would all turn around. But in the heat of the summer, tempers started flaring. An argument between two factory workers from the 46th Street wholesale plant lead to a stabbing, death, and arrest, sending shock waves throughout the facility and the city. While Helmer was not directly responsible for this murder, the tide of affection had started to turn against him as people began to see him as the indirect cause of suffering. The underlying fabric of the organization had never been weaker.

Meanwhile, Helmer was intimately involved in "exclusively" negotiating deals with Michael Shah of DelShah Capital, and simultaneously with Isaac Khafif of the MKF Group, another esteemed real estate developer in Manhattan that had an interest in the building. While secretly working out "exclusive" deals with each of them to drive up the bid price and save the factory and retail store, he was also trying to forge a separate deal with Michael Kraus of Krest Capital, a venture capital fund introduced to him by Marc Halpern.

Ashkenazy Acquisitions was another interested, financial player that Helmer had promised exclusive negotiations with, often bad mouthing the other financiers he was speaking with. Helmer viewed the competition between these major New York City financiers as a way to gain additional leverage in his negotiations. He carefully studied the dynamics of the market and identified major sources of competition. He always made it a point to mention the names of specific, interested investors when sitting down with their competition, in the hopes of staging a bidding war where he would be the ultimate beneficiary.

In the midst of those negotiations, Marcus got a frantic call from the corporate office, which was now located at the remaining West 46th Street facility.

"Marcus, agents from the Labor Department are here with a warrant. They are demanding to see the books and records. They want Helmer here now."

What had occurred was that the worker's union had finally organized a sit in, demanding their three weeks of back pay. They called in the Department of Labor to assist, despite being a union shop. Years earlier, when the possibility that the Baker's Union was going to unionize H&H, Helmer came up with a brilliant plan to frustrate their efforts and insure he remained in control of the workers. He did this by inviting the Tobacco Union to set up shop at H&H. In this way, the Baker's Union had no choice but to defer to their fellow brotherhood in unionizing the shop. But the Tobacco Union was weak in this geographic area and would be no trouble for Helmer to deal with. The Department of Labor was a different story, however. The

Department of Labor could refer this matter to the District Attorney's office, and they could convert it to a criminal case, and in light of Helmer's prior history, this was likely to be the outcome.

When Marcus and Helmer pulled up in the Mini-Cooper, there was a gathering of angry workers outside the plant. Marcus could sense their affinity for Helmer was fading, if not already faded. They were yelling to Helmer in Spanish, asking when they were going to get paid.

Helmer and Marcus made their way through the crowd to the upstairs offices. Helmer was mumbling under his breath something Marcus only heard him say when he was really stressed, "Dios Mio".

The halls and the corporate office were filled with angry workers. When Marcus and Helmer entered their own office, an agent from the investigation and enforcement unit of the Department of Labor greeted them.

"Mr. Toro? I am here because we have a complaint that these workers haven't been paid for three weeks?"

"Well. I will have to look into that."

"Look into it? They either have or they haven't been paid."

"I'll have to check with the accountants."

"They also say they received no written confirmation of their hours worked, their rate of pay, or the amount due to them after withholdings."

"I will definitely look into that."

"Okay, we will wait for you while you do."

Marcus could see Helmer was nervous, but he was trying to put on his best game face. Hiding behind professionals, comptrollers, and managers was a common approach Helmer used to buy time in every crisis. He tried to portray himself as only remotely involved in the business' happenings, as opposed to being directly involved. He thought it created an impression of plausible deniability.

"How about I offer everyone a bagel and orange juice while they are waiting?"

"Mr. Toro, they don't want a bagel. They want to be paid."

"What about you? Would you like a bagel?"

"No, Mr. Toro. I want these workers to be paid."

Helmer then went through the motions of pretending he was investigating the payroll records of the employees. He was squinting and running his finger down the ledger page like he was actually unsure of the fact that no one had been paid in three pay periods. It was all an elaborate charade because he clearly knew the facts. While doing this, Marcus could see that Helmer's mental computer was feverishly working to devise a plan to keep the matter from becoming criminal. He needed to buy some time with the workers and the Department of Labor. His solution was among the most calculated, cunning, and diabolical things Marcus had ever witnessed.

The formulation and execution of this plan was a defining moment for Marcus. He knew at this point he needed to separate himself from H&H and Helmer, or the consequences could be dire for him and his family.

After some time of staring at the ledger books, Helmer confidently proceeded to execute his scheme. He directed the accounting department to issue checks to all the workers for their three weeks of back pay. He then presented copies of those checks to the Department of Labor and began to call the workers in to receive their checks, apologizing for the delay and explaining it was that the accounting department was so busy working with the Bankruptcy Court that it had fallen behind in its normal work, like payroll. This elaborate showcase managed to get the Department of Labor to withdraw its agents and vacate the premises with the warning that they would be monitoring the situation closely, and they would be back if necessary.

Upon the Labor Department's departure, Helmer directed each of the workers to simultaneously go to a specifically assigned check cashing establishment to cash their checks. He admonished them to go to only the location assigned to them and to go immediately. He had meticulously mapped out every single check cashing location in Manhattan and the surrounding boroughs. Helmer knew that there was no money in the payroll account, but he accurately predicted that if all the workers went simultaneously to different locations they would be able to cash their checks before the establishments figured out that they were bad.

While this scheme bought him a whole new set of legal problems, it eliminated the issue of his workers walking off the job, and kept the Department of Labor from turning the matter over to the District Attorney's office. What it also did was cost Helmer the support and employment of Marcus, who packed his things and resigned from his position as National Business Manager that day over Helmer's protests. He could no longer be party to the escalating deception and unscrupulous dealings that was dismantling the H&H organization. Marcus made his way through the crowd of employees, waiting in line for their phony paychecks, and headed home.

Chapter 21

November 2011- Marcus' phone rang and he recognized the number. It was Sumathi Reddy, a renowned reporter from **The Wall Street Journal**. She had covered the H&H downfall for over the course of the past year and a half.

"This is Marcus."

"Hi, Marcus. It's Sumathi Reddy from **The Wall Street Journal**. Do you remember me?"

"Of course. How are you?"

"Good, thanks. I was wondering if you had any comment on the recent motion filed by Helmer and Amy Toro to stop the sale of the remaining H&H property?"

"I haven't seen it, and quite honestly, I don't work there anymore so I it does not concern me."

"I think you should take a look at it. It actually is all about you."

"What? What do you mean?"

"Listen, you have my number. Why don't you read it and call me back."

"Can you send it to me because it probably isn't online yet and I can't make it to the Clerk's office."

"Okay. Sending it now. Call me after."

Helmer and Amy Toro had submitted a motion to the Federal Bankruptcy Court demanding that the auction sale be stayed because they had uncovered that they were the victims of an unscrupulous and manipulative National Business Manager that led them astray.

While Marcus shouldn't have been surprised, he found himself trembling as he read this well-crafted fairytale.

The motion included articles and news clippings about Marcus' legal troubles in order to make it more convincing. The allegations were that this charlatan, namely Marcus, had convinced Helmer to become involved with shady mortgage providers who would eventually try to wrestle his empire from him. The motion portrayed Helmer as the successful but gullible son of a sugar cane farmer that fell victim to a manipulating schemer, that Helmer later learned had a criminal record. His detrimental reliance on this now terminated National Business Manager is what allegedly caused the total and complete financial decimation of H&H and its related companies.

"Wow," Marcus said out loud.

Amy had told Marcus on numerous occasions that Helmer was a sociopath. She claimed he had no conscience and that he would climb over anyone to get what he wanted. He was no psychologist, but she may have been right. Marcus was furious. No one did more to help Helmer personally and professionally than Marcus. Helmer had been deeply entrenched in the foreclosures on the mortgages in question when he met Marcus at Rikers. The notion that he didn't know Marcus' history was laughable considering where they had met. But Marcus conceded that it made a compelling story, and true to form for the man who never took responsibility for his actions during the entire time Marcus knew him.

For Marcus, the greatest disappointment was the recognition that the kindness Helmer showed him by offering him the H&H job was, like all of Helmer's "good deeds," completely and totally self-serving. Marcus knew he was just another pawn in Helmer's chess game.

While the tale of "Helmer the victim" did little to stop the bankruptcy auction, it did insure that Marcus would never wittingly have communication with Helmer again. Their only interaction would be that coincidental meeting on a crowded New York City subway car in the heat of the summer of 2014.

Chapter 22

"Loxed Out: H&H Bagel Evicted From Last Site" (Sumathi Reddy, **The Wall Street Journal**)

Such was the headline in **The Wall Street Journal**, with similar headlines posted across the other major news outlets on January 27, 2012. The efforts of Helmer Toro to hold others accountable for the complications that led to the demise of H&H fell on deaf ears. Tolerance, sympathy, and legal avenues had all been exhausted in the two years of battles to try to save the H&H companies.

On January 26, 2012, the City Marshal, on behalf of the Bankruptcy Trustee, seized the realty property at 639 W. 46th Street, NY, NY and evicted the wholesale, retail, and corporate divisions of H&H Bagels to make way for Isaac Khafif and MKF. Khafif, the successful bidder at auction held on January 4, 2012, had decided to take the control of the building and eradicate himself of the baggage brought by

Helmer Toro and his legacy. H&H was no longer part of his renovation plans for the building, nor was any relationship with Toro.

Once the building and store were vacated, the only thing left to talk about was money. Real estate, mortgages, leases, equipment financing, bagel sales, and employment records all ceased to have any significance, except that all these matters related to how much money the H&H creditors would receive from the finite sum that would be left after the auction sale. This was the only issue at hand.

After the sale of the building there remained, approximately, $11,000,000 to be divided among the numerous creditors, trustees, lawyers, and other interested parties. As with all things involving Helmer Toro, the matter of distribution of this sum was not easily settled. Years of litigation, claims, cross-claims, and counter claims would ensue.

Well into the summer of 2015, a full 3.5 years after the auction sale, that sum remained undisbursed, as secured and unsecured creditors continued to fight over priority, and the Toros battled with the IRS to release Amy Toro from any liability for the sizable tax debt.

The largest secured creditor was the U.S. Government, claiming $22,000,000 on behalf of the American taxpayers. The first mortgagee on the building followed behind with a claim of approximately $11,000,000. The legal and administrative fees for having to deal with the onslaught of motions brought by Helmer and Amy Toro amounted to almost $2,000,000. Miscellaneous creditors including New York State, Wilenta Feed, and others accounted for another substantial amount of money. Oddly, of all of the hundreds of employees of H&H that were unpaid when the operations ceased doing business, only two filed claims for their back wages. Those employees were Marcus, and long-time Sales Manager, Norman Levy.

Chapter 23

"Alas, H&H Bagels Are NOT Headed To Downtown Manhattan"- (**The Gothamist**)

August 2012- If the study of H&H Bagels teaches one lesson that is worth noting, it is the unbelievable power of a respected brand in the marketplace. Once a brand takes hold with the American public, it becomes indelibly ingrained in the American culture and psyche. The more powerful a brand becomes, the more people want to be associated with it. It takes on a self-perpetuating, forward momentum that is very difficult to suppress. The value of the H&H brand was more valuable, perhaps, than all of the tangible assets Helmer had amassed. To some degree, Helmer had this right. A study of the life and death of H&H is the quintessential study of branding power.

Stories began to break, in the summer of 2012, about the resurgence of an H&H retail operation in the Wall Street area. The news media and consumers welcomed this news with excitement, anticipation, and curiosity. Marcus saw the headlines and scratched his head as well.

"How can that be," he thought to himself.

According to reports, Helmer Toro had made a licensing deal with Randy Narod, the affluent owner of the Long Island Bagel Café chain to open a Wall Street location to be named, "The Original H&H Bagels." News reports and speculation varied about Toro's financial involvement in the venture, but most suggested that it must be significant.

No sooner did the story break than other financial stakeholders came forward to claim that they were the rightful holders of the "H&H" name and intellectual property, many with claims founded on legitimate grounds.

These claimants included Harry Abrams, a financier that had lent Helmer money in exchange for a collateral assignment of the name and trademark. After Helmer defaulted, Abrams claimed that he was now the rightful owner of the brand.

There was also the very familiar, Robert Benjamin, who claimed, as part of his multi-million dollar judgment against, and settlement with the Toros, that he was the rightful holder of the "H&H" intellectual property and name.

Finally, there was the Internal Revue Service, who claimed they had seized the intellectual property, held by the Fourth Toro, a non-Bankruptcy protected entity and corporate holder of the intellectual property. They publically warned any party or entity of the consequences of proceeding to use the name H&H Bagels without their express permission, still being owed more than $11,000,000.

Regardless of who was correct, the deal fell apart in August 2012, with Helmer Toro taking to the media to besmirch Narod as a shady businessman that was trying to best him of his rightful property. Helmer was always the victim. The store opened eventually under the name 125 Fulton Street Bagels, with no involvement from Toro, at all.

While the new, "Original H&H" did not come to pass, it demonstrated for Marcus, who had become nostalgic about the brand, the unbelievable fortitude and self-destruction that it took for one man to single-handedly destroy the most recognized, beloved, and interesting brand in the bagel business.

Epilogue

May 2015- Marcus walked past the Coronado on his way to the subway when heard a familiar, shrill voice calling out his name.

"Marcus, Marcus…Marcus!"

He couldn't believe his eyes, or his ears. He knew, instantly, who it was. It was Dr. Amy Dukoff-Toro. She was racing towards him now.

"Marcus. You tell Helmer when you speak to him-"

He instantly cut her off.

"Amy, I don't speak to Helmer and I haven't in years."

Apparently, as Marcus understood it, the Toros were getting a divorce and Helmer had relocated to Puerto Rico, probably looking for investors for a new project.

"Well if you do speak with him-"

He cut her off again.

"Amy, I am not going to speak with him. He is a bad man and my life is better without him. All I care about now is getting my money. Take care. I have to catch a train."

"Well what about the creditors? They need to stop suing me. I have nothing to do-"

"Amy, I don't speak to the creditors. It has been 4 years since this has had anything to do with me. Take care."

With that, Marcus raced for his train and he thought to himself, "No one would ever believe this story if I tried to tell it. They would be sure I was making it all up. These things just don't happen in real life."

THE END

SD - #0014 - 070726 - C0 - 203/127/8 - PB - 9780692542835 - Gloss Lamination